SCENES FROM THE PAST 14

W0006013

RAILWAYS OF NORTH WALES

BANGOR

Bangor. 9th July 1948. The Down 'Irish Mail' runs through the Down Fast line on the final leg of its journey from Euston to Holyhead. The locomotive, No.**46127** *Old Contemptibles*, of Holyhead Shed (7C), had acquired its new London Midland Region number, but retained the post-war livery of black, lined out in straw with a maroon band whilst the tender still proclaimed its previous owners. No.2 signalbox behind the locomotive was built into the embankment, and the location of the old name-board, removed at the outbreak of World War Two, can clearly be seen.   *J.M. Dunn.*

BILL REAR

First Published by Foxline Publishing 1992

ISBN 978 1 907094 81 1

Reprinted June 2012 by Booklaw Publications, 382 Carlton Hill, Nottingham, NG4 1JA

Printed by The Amedeus Press, Cleckheaton, West Yorkshire, BD19 4TQ

(frontispiece) **Bangor (Motive Power Yard).** Jubilee Class 4-6-0 No.**45556** *Nova Scotia* stands on the coaling road being prepared by its traincrew. This low viewpoint, taken inside the 60ft diameter turntable pit shows the graceful lines of these locomotives to good advantage. *Norman Kneale.*

BANGOR

Geographical & Historical

Bangor was the first western terminus of the Chester & Holyhead Railway and was opened with the Saltney Junction to Bangor section of the line on 1st May 1848 with four trains each way daily. Freight traffic started the following month. The original station was designed by Francis Thompson and built by a Mr Morris of Birkenhead. It remained the terminus of the line for nearly two years whilst construction of the Britannia Tubular Bridge continued. The first through trains started running between Holyhead and Euston on 18th March 1850 when the 2.30pm express was the first public passenger train to traverse the whole of the CHR. The Down tube of the bridge opened on 19th October the same year. From the outset, the London & North Western Railway ran the services on behalf of the Chester & Holyhead Railway. The C&HR was eventually absorbed by the LNWR on 1st January 1859.

Bangor station site spanned a shallow valley, and was very restricted, being hemmed in between two hills. The line tunnelled through Bangor mountain (913yds) to the east, and westward through Belmont tunnel (726yds, shortened to 615 yds). Into this confined area were crammed the passenger station, freight facilities, Motive Power and Civil Engineers Departments. On the LNWR track plan dated 1876, the main Up and Down lines opened out to four roads through the station before converging at their respective tunnel-mouths. At the eastern end, the four tracks crossed Caernarvon Road, a factor which inhibited development at the site, and necessitated extending and duplicating the bridge over the road. As originally constructed, the station had two main platforms west of the road bridge.

On the Down side, a narrow ticket platform adjoined Bangor tunnel-mouth and next to its ramp was East Signal Box, which controlled movements leading to and from the platform lines where the two roads widened to four. The Down platform had one through road and a bay line at the Holyhead end on the opposite face. The original goods warehouse adjoined the platform. This had one track into the building with a second terminating outside, these two warehouse lines containing small wagon turntables linked by a short length of track. A third siding extended into the yard whilst a fourth line ended alongside cattle pens. A road access was provided from Caernarvon Road into the goods yard, but which was subsequently closed to make way for extensions. On the opposite side of this road access was the loco shed and yard, containing a five road engine shed which was subsequently converted into the goods warehouse. Between the engine shed and the ramp were three sidings. On the far side of the engine shed was a 36ft turntable, with five short sidings of varying length, and an access road off the No.1. shed road. The turntable was extended in 1859 to 40ft. A second access point off Caernarvon Road led to the coal yard beyond the engine shed, in which

were four stock sidings and another siding adjoining the weighing machine and weigh office. The Civil Engineers yard had its workshops at the Caernarfon end of the site, alongside which was a single rail access which opened out to two sidings in the Engineers Yard. The whole complex on the Down side converged at Belmont tunnel-mouth, and necessitated most shunting and positioning movements entering Belmont tunnel.

On the Up side, on emerging from Belmont tunnel, Bangor signal cabin was located near the tunnel-mouth. Immediately east of the signal box the formation widened to the main platform road, which was stepped at the Holyhead end to provide a short trailing spur where stock for attaching to the rear of Up trains could stand, enabling rapid attachment to be made. The platform road extended beyond the converging points at the eastern end to a short siding. There was a bay platform at the Holyhead end used by local trains, with two stock sidings parallel to the bay line, a short horse landing and a single road carriage shed which held three vehicles, and which had been installed by April 1848. The shed was reported as having been blown down in September 1849. Access to the carriage shed was off the Up line in front of the signal box and from the shunting neck which passed behind the cabin.

As early as 1852, improvements were found to be necessary and these were made to the booking offices and waiting rooms. Also included was the track-work at the station and extensions to the goods warehouse. Despite these improvements the increasing traffic activity was still hampered by the restricted site, and to ease shunting operations, authority was obtained to open out 135 yards of Belmont tunnel in 1881. The following year saw the bridge over Caernarvon Road widened, which permitted the lengthening of the Up platform. Despite the opening out of the tunnel-mouth, shunting still necessitated engines going into one or the other tunnels, an operation which persisted until the demise of freight traffic which coincided with the end of steam. The developing branch lines, increasing frequency and loading of trains placed severe strain on the Motive Power Department, partially hampered by the nature of the site, and consequently F.W. Webb, the Chief Mechanical Engineer, agreed to provide a new shed with traditional LNWR northlight pattern roof to house 24 locomotives, together with combined tank (capacity 70,331 gallons) above a coal stage with a new 42ft. turntable alongside, a development which was opened in 1884 on its present site. The Goods Department took over the former M.P.D. depot and modified it to suit its needs. Some improvements were made to the Motive Power department buildings during 1920, when new offices were reported as under construction on 16th June. At the time of writing, both buildings still stand although the latter Motive Power Depot is not now in railway use although the

Goods Warehouse is used by the Engineering Department. Traffic continued to increase steadily and at the 1923 Grouping, was still inhibited by the restricted site. The newly formed London, Midland and Scottish Railway implemented improvements which were commenced in 1924 and completed by 1927. This involved reconstruction of the Up platform into an island configuration, providing an extra platform face on the former station entrance side by extending the bay platform at the Holyhead end into a through road, together with a parallel Up goods line. A short facing siding into a horse landing led off the Up goods loop. A second bridge was constructed over Caernarvon Road to carry the new Up Goods and Passenger Loop lines which converged at Bangor tunnel mouth. The front of the original station buildings was retained upon rebuilding in 1924. The original Chester & Holyhead Railway monograms were carved in stone and mounted in the walls of the original building on the Up platform side at the time of construction, a feature which was retained when the station was enlarged, and still clearly visible to this day. A new building was constructed in the original station forecourt comprising booking hall, parcels and left luggage offices. Access to the platforms from ground level was by a double staircase leading to the overbridge which traversed the tracks and gave access to the two island platforms. Electric luggage lifts were incorporated in each platform and the forecourt, enabling luggage trolleys to be moved in safety. A short length bay platform was built into the modified Down passenger loop line at the Chester end, specifically for the Bethesda service, which was worked by motor train. The former No.1. signal cabin, located on

the Down platform, was replaced by a new larger structure with an eighty-two lever LNWR tappet frame, whilst No.2. signal box at the Holyhead end of the site was replaced by an enlarged structure west of the original box and contained a ninety lever tappet frame. At the time of reconstruction in 1924, the lighting throughout was changed from gas to electric and the open fireplaces in offices and waiting rooms were replaced by central heating operated by three separate boilers. A new water tank with capacity of 61,262 gallons, together with water pump, treatment plant and filter equipment was built alongside the new No.1. signal box. This drew its supply from a catchment pit at Felin Hen on the Bethesda branch, and supplied the shed tank over the Coal Stage, the Yard Crane and the columns on the platforms, Bethesda Bay and the Up and Down Passenger Loop lines. Alternative supplies were available from Bangor Corporation. The differences in height between the catchment pit and the tank on the station site was minimal, and the supply from Felin Hen was frequently blocked.

Fully licenced refreshment rooms were provided on both Up and Down platforms, under the control of a manageress. Living accommodation for the staff was provided over the rooms on the Up platform.

Traffic Department

Traffic was under the supervision of Bangor Station-master, who also was responsible for signal boxes at Bethesda Junction and Penrhyn Siding. In 1953, traffic staff totalled 52 persons, excluding two District Traffic Inspectors and two Railway Service Repre-

No.1. Bangor. 1947. A familiar view of Bangor, taken in the last summer of the LMS. Smoke drifts across the western end of the station from the Motive power Depot whilst an unidentified 0-6-0 shunts wagons in the Engineers Yard. An LNW 0-6-2T makes its way on the Down Carriage Siding alongside stock on the Down Platform Loop, probably to attach to the two coaches standing in the Bethesda Bay. Sundry permanent way materials are stacked between the water tank and the bridge abutment, whilst a wagon of rubble stands in front of the tank in the short siding behind No.1. signal box. Coaching stock stands in both Up platform faces, with more on the Up Goods Loop. Both platform canopies covering the subway under the tracks are under repair, replacing glass panels which were removed for safe keeping at the commencement of World War Two. *G.H. Platt.*

sentatives who were attached to the staff of the District Traffic Superintendent at Chester. Carriage cleaning also came under the supervision of the station-master who had ten cleaners attending to the exterior and interior demands of passenger rolling stock. There was one wagon examiner resident at that time, although for many years a wagon repair shop was located at the west end of the station on the Down side, under the shade of the excavated cutting by Belmont tunnel. A Telegraph Office was located on the station and dealt with internal railway and postal telegrams and reported train movements to Control. The Passenger Agent staff comprised four booking and four parcels clerks and two motor parcels van men.

Goods Department

The Goods Department consisted of a warehouse, which still stands to this day, although not on its original location but on the site of the first locomotive shed. It was latterly used as a road haulage depot, but when in railway use contained two roads holding nine wagons each, together with loading docks. The yard alongside had three sidings which included one for a coal. Goods was received and delivered to and from the yard, and four motor vehicles and four mechanical horses and trailers were in use. The Goods Department staff consisted of forty persons in 1953. Merchandise traffic amounted to 19095 tons received in 5663 wagons, and 21060 tons of mineral traffic in 2860 wagons was

forwarded. A total of 5772 wagons of merchandise amounting to 18426 tons, and 2530 wagons of minerals, amounting to 22717 tons, was received. Outgoing minerals from Bangor consisted mainly of slate products, some of which was a form of slate dust known as fullersite, originating from Bethesda district. This traffic was loaded at Port Penrhyn, having been brought from Bethesda by the Penrhyn Quarries own narrow gauge railway, where it was transhipped. Bangor was also the tranship point dealing with traffic for Anglesey, and was a Zonal Centre for delivery and collection of traffic within a ten mile radius.

Engineering Department

Originally, the Engineer responsible for the permanent way and works for the North Wales district, which included Dublin and Wirral for quite some time, had offices on the first floor of the station building. The area south of the goods shed was subsequently developed to provide new offices and workshops for the District Engineers department. The Civil Engineers complex consisted of Technical and General Offices which administered the whole of the civil engineering work in the district, including all the main and branch lines between Holyhead and Chester. Upon nationalisation, it also assumed control of the former Mersey Railway, the Wirral line to West Kirby and the Cheshire Lines Committee line from Chester to Wrexham. The workshops were chiefly concerned with maintenance and renewal of stations,

No.2. Bangor. 1947. On the hillside above No.2. signal box, a fine panorama of the station, Motive Power, Goods Yard and Engineer's complex could be seen, but access was difficult, and few people took the trouble to make the trip. From left to right, the passenger station complex, showing the lift towers on the Up and Down island platforms connected by a dual purpose bridge for passengers and trolleys that connected with the 1924 Booking Hall and forecourt, just out of view. Notice the walk way boards covering the point rodding and signal wires between the Down Fast and platform roads that extended from No.2 signal box. Immediately right of the platform roads is the motive power yard, adjoining that are two carriage siding and two goods shed roads. The goods shed is approximately centre picture. This was the first engine shed, and its origins are clearly defined. The building was modified when the replacement shed came into use. In the lower right can be seen the Engineer's yard, which included the Permanent Way Department. All tracks converge at the eastern end of the station below the photographer. It will be appreciated just how difficult it was to ensure that engines coming off shed to take up their duties were released without blocking main line traffic. Frequently traffic density on the main lines was such that it could take half an hour to release and engine, thus compounding the issue.   *J.M. Dunn.*

buildings, bridges, docks and harbours, but not the maintenance of the permanent way apart from supplying tools. At one time the District Engineer had his own locomotive and Inspection saloon. The first engine to be built at Crewe Works, the old Alexander Allan Single engine "*Columbine*", after withdrawal from revenue earning service in 1902, was allocated to the District Engineer, Bangor, and carried the nameplate "*ENGINEER BANGOR*". Its predecessor was the engine formerly named "*Dwarf*", which it replaced in November 1877. Within the Engineering Department complex were Joiners Shop, Smithy, Saw-mill, Wood-working machine shop, Building and Station Stores and a Mortar Mill. Until the general decline set in, in the late 1950s, the staff engaged in the Engineering Department totalled 260 persons. With the decline in traffic following the closure of the branch lines, the department and workshop role diminished, but survived until 1966 when the final sixty members of staff lost their jobs or were transferred to other areas. The reorganisation reduced the District status to an Area Office. The buildings survived for some time, but eventually they too were demolished. At the time of writing (January 1992), there is an Engineering presence, ironically housed in the original station offices over No.1. platform. Many of the tracks in the Permanent Way yard were removed, but one or two sidings survive.

Other departments with a presence at Bangor were the Signal and Telegraph department, with two linesmen and four assistants, and a Police Department with two officers.

Social Issues

The railway was obliged to provide accommodation for its staff from early days, and the LNWR built a small estate of 76 houses to the usual Crewe pattern. The estate was adjoining the station site on the south side.

As was the custom amongst large organisations, social activity and staff welfare was an issue that presented itself, and after representations to the LNWR over a period of years, eventually the Company provided land, a building and facilities, known as the Bangor Railway Institute in the Euston Road. It was built by the LNWR and constructed partially from materials that were removed from the original station at Llandudno Junction. The building was formerly opened by the Chairman of the LNWR, Lord Stalbridge, on 7th December 1898, and available to all railway employees, its Committee being charged a nominal rent of one guinea per annum, which included a supply of coal for heating purposes. The agreement was slightly revised on 15th February 1900 with a stipulation that 15 tons of coal per annum was to be supplied for heating. In 1906 the Railway Company made an extension to the premises to accommodate two billiard tables. A new agreement was signed on 6th March of the same year which provided for the rent of £26. 1s. 0d to be paid, and rates, by the members. The Landlord, as before, provided 15 tons of coal per annum, and all gas required. A Social Club adjoining the Billiard Room was opened on 1st July 1925 and on 10th November the same year, the Agreement was modified for the Tenant to pay the Landlord for all electric current consumed over and above a cost of £15 per annum. Due to the recession and the financial position of the Railway Company (by now the LMS), the Agreement was

modified and the Institute Committee became responsible for the whole cost of fuel and lighting. Things improved slightly and the President wrote to Mr Darbyshire (for the Railway Company) on 14th May 1937, on behalf of the Committee, agreeing structural alterations and improvements for the Social Club and new accommodation, the work to be financed and carried out by the Railway Company, at an estimated cost of £300, the Committee to repay the costs incurred at a rate of 3% per annum for 12 years. At some stage, no doubt to provide extra revenue, outside members were admitted, and at the A.G.M. in March 1948, it was reported that membership comprised 517 railway and 106 outside members. J. M. Dunn visited the building in May 1950 and was shown round the premises. Facilities included a Concert Hall, down one side of which was a Gauge "0" model railway which had been for the instruction of Traffic and Locomotive Mutual Improvement Classes, but was by now not in use. In the Billiards Room, which housed two full sized tables, was a model of a cast-iron bridge which Robert Stephenson originally intended to build across the Menai Straits, and had belonged to one of the Directors of the Chester & Holyhead Railway. The Secretarys Office housed a library of books, whose subjects ranged from fiction to travel and with a special section of railway interest. The only room that showed signs of regular activity was the bar, which even in those days had a turnover of £10,000. With the decline of the railway involvement at Bangor, Institute membership declined and eventually closed but the exact date is not known. At the time of the opening of the Railway Institute, a Railway Temperance Hall in Caernarvon Road was provided but few details are known of this facility or how long it survived.

J. M. Dunn under-earthed a little-known issue which has a modern day interpretation, raised itself at Bangor in 1895. On 19th June of that year, and reported in Parliament - House of Commons Session 1895 - a Circular, issued by W. Dawson, of the Permanent Way Department at Bangor to its Inspectors, entitled Men unable to speak English, reads as follows:

> *Notwithstanding my instructions on this subject, I find that a number of men have been taken on who cannot speak English or who can only speak English a little.*
>
> *The services of all such men are to be dispensed with as it is contrary to the Cs rules to have them in their employ. Let me know which of the men you can dispense with first.*
>
> *I do not wish you to serve all the men with a weeks notice at once, but they must be paid off gradually, unless they learn to speak English in the meantime. Let me have your report upon the subject before the end of the month.*

Mr Dawson wrote again on 6th July to his Inspectors as follows:

> *Having reference to my circular of 19th. ultimo., you understand that the list you are to send in is to*

include every man who cannot speak English and every man who can only speak English a little.
I shall afterwards examine many of the men myself, so that I hope you will take such steps as to ensure your list being quite correct.
If necessary, send me a revised list marking in red ink those which you can dispense with first. If the list you have already sent me is correct, you had better let me have a letter concerning this.

Mr Dunn observed At the same time that the Welsh speaking controversy was in full swing, Lloyd George was standing for Parliament in the Bangor constituency and as the L.N.W.R. Engineering Department employed a large proportion of the male members of the population, he was anxious to do what he could to secure their interest. He therefore approached the Engineer at Bangor, Mr Cooil, who was one of the leading officials, and asked if the men could be influenced on his behalf. Cooil said he would not bring any pressure to bear on the men to vote in **his** favour but, after a lot of wrangling, promised that he would do nothing to dissuade them, if they felt so minded. In return for this, Lloyd George promised that if he "got in" he would tell Cooil how to settle "that English Welsh business" and so they parted.

In due course Lloyd George did "get in" and also in due course Cooil met Lloyd George in the street and asked him, now that he had been elected, what about the cure for the English Welsh business? Lloyd George hummed and ha'ad and pretended he didn't know what Cooil meant and after the latter explained, the former said "Oh! That! Tut tut! - Election promises! - Election promises!" At that, Cooil walked off in disgust and never spoke to Lloyd George again.

This anecdote was told to J.M. Dunn by Mr Cooil, son of the Engineer, and also of the Engineering Department at Bangor in June 1948.

The matter was referred to in *The Railway Magazine* for December 1903 in a report on the LNWR progress with the scheme for widening the Chester and Holyhead line between Chester and Llandudno Junction. The passage is lengthy and not directly relevant to this matter, apart from a sentence in the middle of the passage dealing with the Bill submitted for an Act of Parliament authorising the new works. It reads:

*The traffic had become so congested that some years since it was decided to duplicate a portion of the line A Bill for this purpose was introduced in Parliament, **but was withdrawn owing to the dispute of the company with the Welsh-speaking servants and the consequent action of Parliament thereon.***

Mr Dunn contacted Lt. Col. D.A. Price White, M.P. on 23rd June 1948 enquiring how he (Dunn) might acquire a copy of the Hansard Debate which dealt with this matter. Some correspon-

dence then ensued between Lt. Col. Price Whites agent and the House of Commons Library, and eventually received a brief reply from Barbara Shuttleworth, a Secretary to the Research assistant at the Library, who incidentally was shot dead two days after writing the reply, by a Polish person! Her reply was very brief. She found no trace of a Bill having been withdrawn but offers Hansard references for the relevant period. These are summarised as follows:

London & North Western Railway Bill
Ordered for Third Reading 2nd April 1895
(Hansard, 4.s. Vol.32. col.764.)

Friday 5th April 1895.
(Hansard, 4.s. Vol.32. col.1023.)
Mr D. Lloyd George moved that the third reading be postponed. Bill put down for following Monday.

25th April 1895.
(Hansard, 4.s. Vol.32. cols. 1605-1610.)
Mr D. Lloyd George objected to debate on Bill until the Directors of the Company had reconsidered their attitude in regard to certain actions of their officers in North Wales on the subject of the weeding-out of Welsh-speaking workmen on the railway. The debate was adjourned for a fortnight.

9th May 1895.
(Hansard, 4.s. Vol.33. cols. 780-785.)
Debate on Third Reading. Bill passed.
Ayes 233, Noes 106.

Royal Assent, 6th July 1895.

The subject re-appeared in an article on the Story of Lloyd George, entitled My brother and I in the *Liverpool Daily Post*, dated Saturday May 17th 1958. The passage is too long to quote in full, but summarised, showed how the new Member of Parliament was aware of parliamentary procedure at a very early stage in his political career, and exploited it on his own behalf, and on behalf of his constituents. The article pointed out that whilst Parliament had no direct jurisdiction over the LNWR, on the other hand the Company could not carry on its business without the help of Parliament, and in previous years the Company had regularly applied to Parliament for larger powers to carry out schemes and improvements. Lloyd George, by proposing a series of amendments to the Companys private Bills going through Parliament, drew the Companys attention to himself. By a series of interviews with the M.P., the Company ascertained what was the root cause of his delaying tactics, and resolved the situation by withdrawing the demand for dispensing with the services of the Welsh speaking servants in return for a smooth passage of their Bill through Parliament!

No.3. Bangor. c.1920. Before the station was rebuilt in 1924, passenger access to the station was up a winding path from Caernarvon Road with the Station Master's house wedged between the path and the bridge. Carriage and motor traffic climbed the steep hill to the forecourt. On rebuilding, the house was demolished, replaced by a second bridge over the road to accommodate the Up Passenger and Goods Loop lines, which merged at Bangor tunnel mouth. *Gwynedd Archives Service.*

No.4. Bangor. c.1920. This interesting view shows Bangor before development and just before the Grouping, taken from above Belmont tunnel looking east. In the right foreground can be seen the Wagon Repair Shop on the Down side, whilst the old No.2. signal box stands between the headshunt and the Up line. A bay platform faces west, used by Amlwch and Caernarfon line trains. An open footbridge straddles the Up and Down platforms, and was replaced during the extensions.
Gwynedd Archives Service.

No.5. Bangor. c.1920. An interesting view looking across the west end of the station towards the Permanent Way Yard, with the District Engineer's Offices prominent in the background. The garden in the foreground was attached to the District Engineer's House. Assorted LNW coaching stock is parked in the bay and Up platform roads, and in the carriage siding between the Down platform and the Motive Power Depot.
Gwynedd Archives Service.

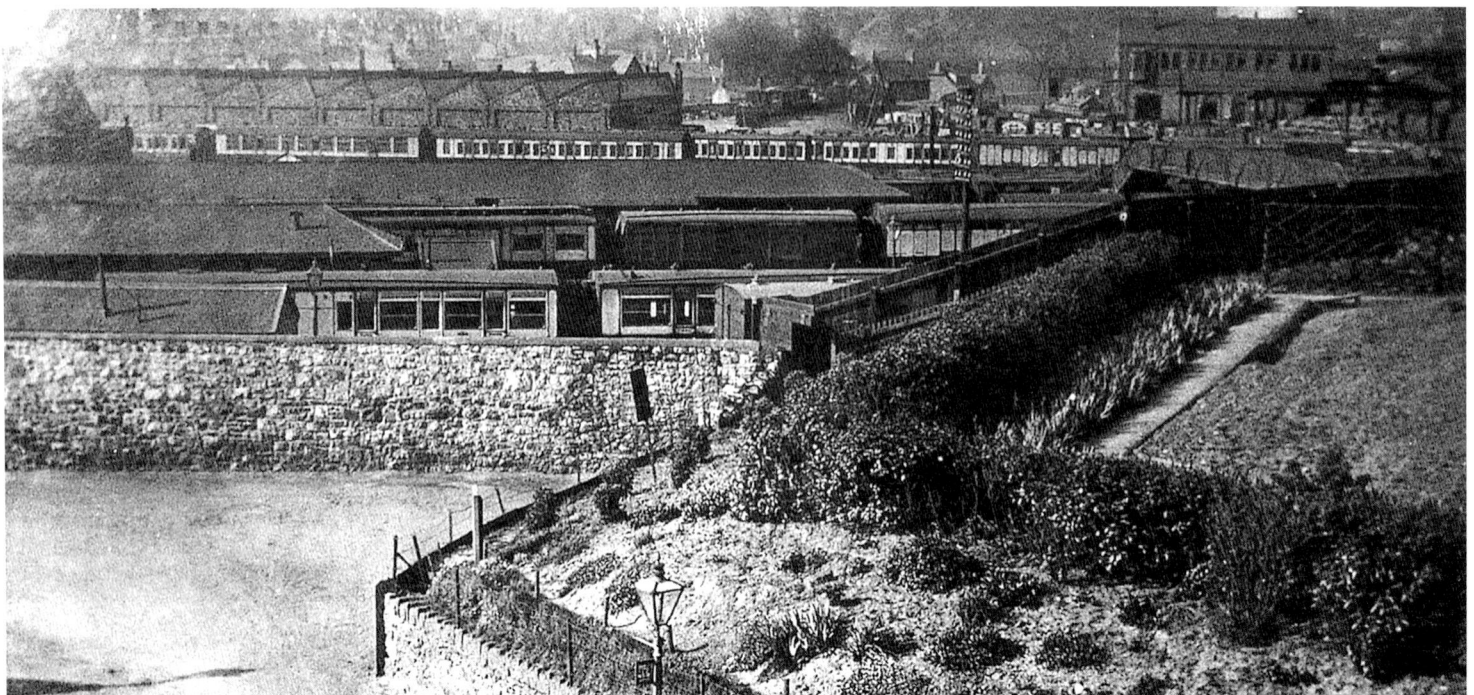

No.6. Bangor. East End. c.1924. Taken from Bangor mountain, looking west, this view shows the redevelopment of the station in its earliest stages, with the site of the Bethesda bay on the Down side resembling a construction site. No.1. signal box in the foreground contains fewer levers than its successor. Note the engine siding on the Up side, where engines taking over Up trains would stand awaiting their duty. The water tank is still on the Up platform, and the Station Master's house stands on Caernarvon Road, both to disappear with the development. The canopy over the Up platform curves towards the West End bay line, giving passengers some shelter when they transfer between branch and main line trains. *Gwynedd Archives Service.*

No.7. Bangor. c.1924. Before rebuilding, the main station entrance was fronted by a long narrow forecourt. The building to the right of the main structure was the parcels and luggage office, and were demolished during rebuilding. On the right hand edge of the picture can be seen the canopy over the West End bay platform, used by Amlwch and Caernarvon local trains. In the background can be seen the locomotive shed, with the smoke vents indicating steam raising activity beneath. Road transport is represented by the solitary car whilst horse drawn drays stand in front of the main station entrance.

Gwynedd Archives Service.

These three pictures form a sequence taken on Bangor station in July 1924 and have been the subject of research to try to establish the relevant workings. The extension work on the station was complete with the Up Loop platform in use, as was the modified Down platform. It is possible the clock shown on the middle photograph is slow, as there were no scheduled arrivals on the Up or Down lines at this time, but ten minutes later, the sequence conforms to known train movements.

No.8. Bangor (East End). LNWR Precursor Class 4-4-0 No.**302** *Greyhound* stands at the head of the 5.25pm from Holyhead to Chester train. It was worked by Bangor men and waited ten minutes before departing all stations to Chester at 6.35pm. In the new short bay platform off the Down Passenger Loop line, the 6.10pm from Bethesda has just arrived, due 6.28pm. The branch was worked as a 'Motor' or push-pull train service, comprising one of the LNW 2-4-2T engines based at Bangor shed. The stock comprised third compartment and driving trailer third coaches, working on circuit 845.

No.9. Bangor (Down platform). Experiment Class 4-6-0 No.**1490** *Wellington* moves slowly along the Down Fast line through the station to the starter, where it will stand until its train arrives from Liverpool. The stock for the 6.35pm to Chester still stands in the Up platform. LNWR colours predominate, although the leading coaches in the formation appear to be in the new LMS livery.

No.10. Bangor (Down platform) Claughton class 4-6-0 No.**37** *G.R. Jebb* stands at the Down platform with the 4.15pm from Liverpool Lime Street to Pwllheli, which comprised through coaches for Afonwen and Holyhead. The telegraph number '397B' does not appear in the Working Time Table for the period, and it is possible that the train was running in two parts, as the 'B' suffix indicates. The Claughton detached and went on shed. The leading four coaches formed the 6.55pm to Afonwen and Pwllheli and was worked by one of Bangor's 0-6-0 tender engines, which generally hauled most of the passenger services over the line at this time. The rear portion was taken on to Holyhead by the Experiment Class loco seen in the previous photograph, and which was standing at the Down Fast Line starter. Following the departure of the Pwllheli train it drew forward into Belmont tunnel and set back onto the stock, depart all stations for Holyhead at 7.00pm. *Collection: J.M. Bentley.*

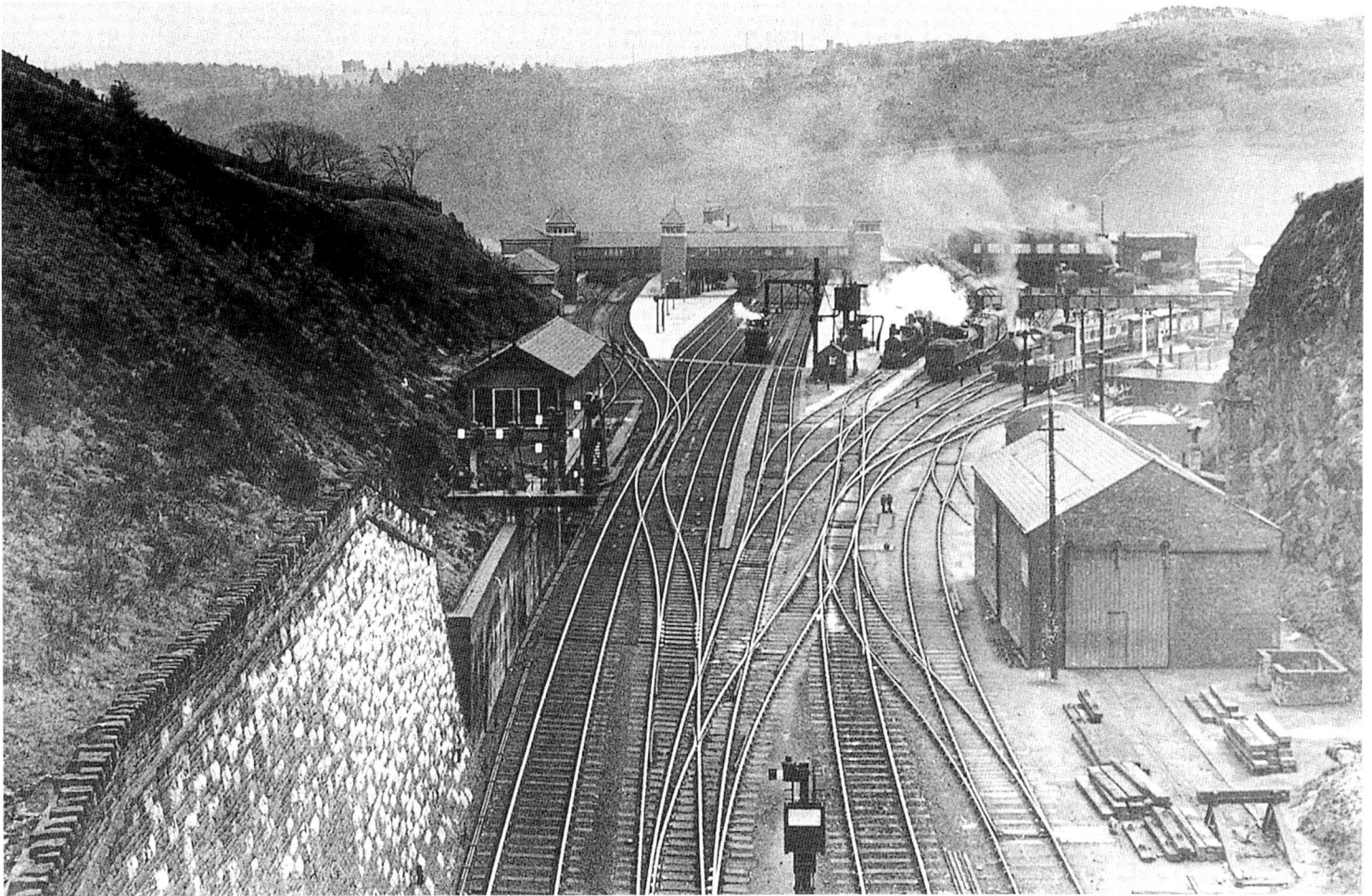

No.11. Bangor. 1926. The extension to Bangor station was largely completed by the date of this photograph, which shows the alterations to the Up platform, creating the new Up Passenger and Goods Loop lines, seen behind the replacement No.2. signal box. In the right foreground can be seen the Wagon Repair Shop. This view emphasises the convergence of lines at Belmont tunnel mouth and the difficulties encountered in slotting engine movements on and off shed into traffic to take up their workings, particularly on summer Saturdays, when main line occupancy was almost continuous.

Collection C.R. Irving in Gwynedd Archives.

No.12. Bangor. 1926. Geo.V. Class 4-4-0 No.**1294** *F.S. Wolferstan* stands on the Up Goods Loop line with a train still in LNWR livery, facing Menai Bridge. The newness of the renovation and extensions stand out, the platform slabs gleaming. The lift towers dominate the scene, and removed the somewhat hazardous procedure involved in moving luggage and parcels across the barrow crossing at the eastern end of the platforms.

Collection C.R. Irving in Gwynedd Archives.

No.13.Bangor. 1926. The modified Up platform, taken from the Down side, showing the original station buildings incorporated into an island platform, and the new passenger and luggage footbridge straddling the tracks.   *Collection C.R. Irving in Gwynedd Archives.*

No.14. Bangor. 1926. The extensions to the station required a new Booking hall to be constructed in the station forecourt, and this imposing structure was the result. The carriage parking area was reduced, but at that time there was little road traffic to cause congestion. The former station building is visible on the left hand side of the picture, now part of the Up side platform.   *Collection C.R. Irving in Gwynedd Archives.*

No.15 Bangor. 1926. Another view of the station exterior, this time taken from the public road. Notice the ornate lamps, and ornamental gates, together with two foot passenger entrances and separate incoming and outgoing vehicular traffic entrances. Just visible beyond the right hand passenger entrance can be seen the Horse Landing beyond the new Parcels Office. *Collection C.R. Irving in Gwynedd Archives.*

No.16 Bangor. The LMS adopted a policy of naming members of the 'Patriot' Class after certain towns served by the Company from about 1937, although selection was somewhat arbitrary. Nevertheless North Wales towns were well represented. In 1938 No.**5523** was named *Bangor* and as was the custom, the naming ceremony took place at the 'home' town. Here members of the public adorn the front buffer beam shortly after the ceremony. *Collection C.R. Irving in Gwynedd Archives.*

No.17. Bangor. 1948. At the eastern end of the station, the main line entered Belmont Tunnel, originally 726 yards in length, but shortened to 615 yards when the station area was enlarged. This view of the eastern portal looking towards Menai Bridge shows the high retaining wall on the Up side, whilst on the Down side a coach stands in the shunting neck. At one time there was a single road wagon repair shop located in this opened out part, but this was removed shortly after the Second World War. Notice the setting -back signal with illuminated road indicator controlling entrance to the various yards on the Down side. This single access point caused congestion and delay throughout the station's history, only eliminated with the closure of the Motive Power, Carriage and Goods Yard facilities. *J.M. Dunn.*

No.18. Bangor Belmont Tunnel. Summer 1964. Princess Coronation Class 4-6-2 No.**46237** *City of Bristol* creeps past the outer home signal and pokes the smokebox into Belmont tunnel on the next stage of the journey to Menai Bridge and Holyhead. The sheer bulk of the pacific coupled with the billowing waves of steam and smoke make an awe-inspiring sight. These locomotives were displaced from the West Coast Main Line, and were cascaded onto the Holyhead route towards the end of their working days. The diagonal stripe across the cab sides proclaim that this locomotive was prohibited from working under the wires, and some of the work they performed was of an lower classification; a year or two earlier and they could not have been spared from the work for which they had been designed. *B.A. Wynne.*

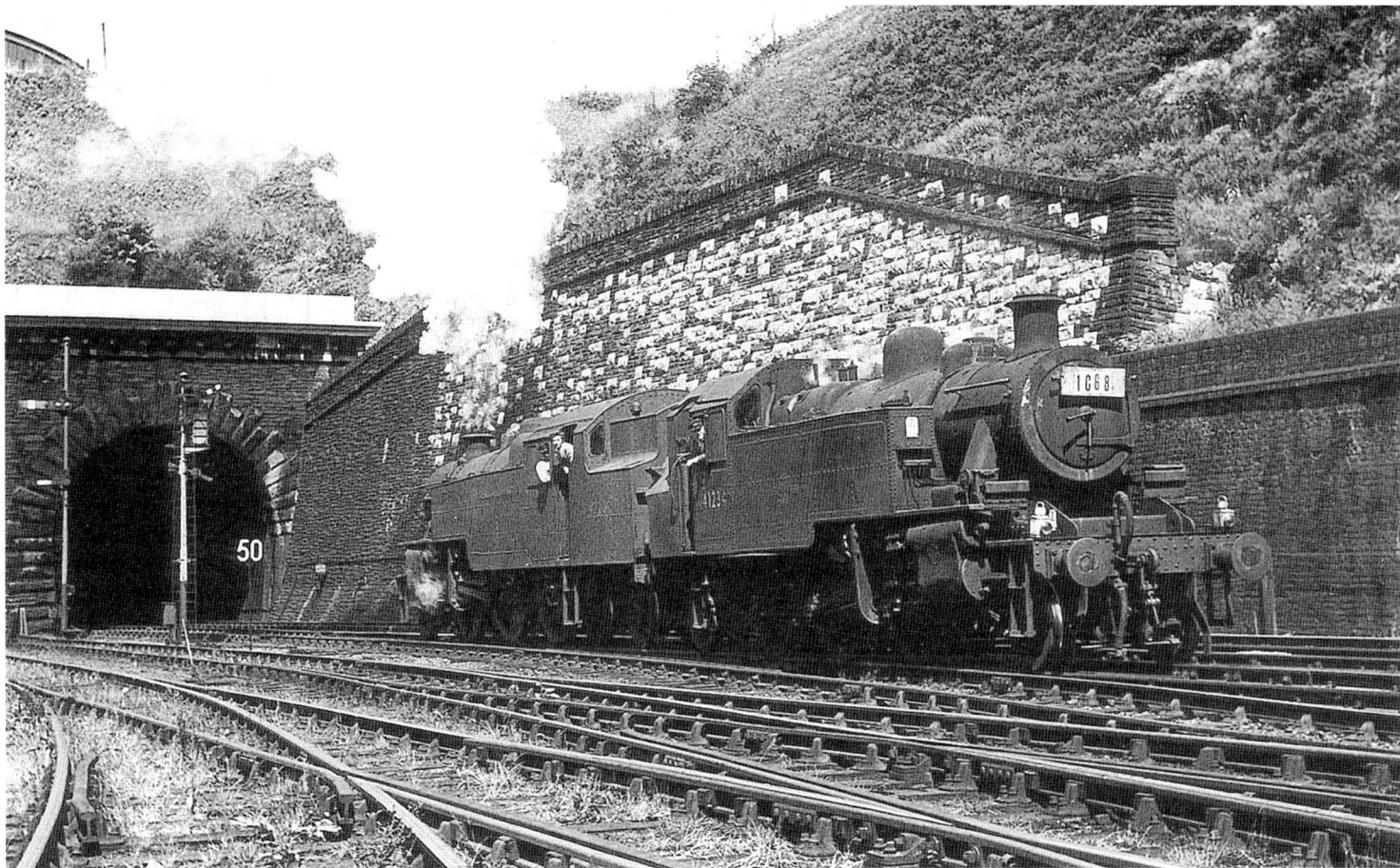

No.19. Bangor (West End). 1964. Reporting number 1C68 was the 9.10am Penychain to Manchester Exchange Saturdays Only working, comprised of ten coaches, which demanded sufficient motive power over the steeply graded Afonwen line. Here Bangor's Class 2MTT 2-6-2 No.**41239** has piloted Fairburn Class 4MTT 2-6-4 No.**42209** on the working to Bangor, where they detached and were replaced by a Class 5 for working forward. The crews would run forward into Bangor tunnel before setting back through the Down fast road through the station, and into Belmont tunnel, when they would reverse and go on shed. Possibly the crews would book off, whilst the engines would be serviced and work a Down train to the holiday camp in the early afternoon. *Norman Kneale.*

No.20. Bangor (West End). c.1964. There was considerable passenger shunting activity throughout the day, as Afonwen line through coaches were combined with Holyhead stock working through to Liverpool Lime Street, Manchester Exchange and Crewe. The station passenger shunt engine was concentrated mainly on Up side workings. For the busier parts of the day a local tank engine was turned off the shed for the purpose. During the quieter periods, engines on standby would undertake the role, and at various times, Holyhead, Llandudno Junction, Chester and Crewe men would find themselves putting an hour on the Up side passenger shunt. Down line workings were usually accommodated on the Passenger Loop platform and after the Holyhead portion had departed, the branch line loco came off the shed to work the stock forward. Here, Ivatt Class 2 2-6-2MTT No **41226** heads towards Belmont tunnel on the Down main line, whilst engaged on station shunt duties. This was one of the vacuum controlled locomotives equipped for push and pull workings, hence the twin vacuum pipes visible on the bunker. *Norman Kneale.*

No.21. Bangor (West End). 1964. The British Railways Standard Class 3 2-6-2T were comparative late-comers to the shed, four of the class having transferred from Machynlleth (89C) in June, painted in Western Region style lined green livery complete with Route Restriction disk displayed below the bunker number. They were popular engines with traincrew, although their sojourn at Bangor was comparatively brief and contact with the engines was, in some cases, minimal. One regular working of these Bangor Class 3 locomotives was 'The Welshman', alias the 10.00am from Porthmadog and Pwllheli to Euston which they worked as far as Bangor, where a Class 6 engine took over for the next stage as far as Chester. Here No.**82033** runs forward to Belmont Tunnel where it will set back and go on shed, after working this duty, signified by the reporting number 1A42 on the bunker. The headlamps indicate a Class '1' working, which is inappropriate for light engine working. *Norman Kneale.*

No.22. Bangor (West End). C.1963. No.2 signal box was set into the hillside at the west end of Bangor, and the front of the signal box was flush with the embankment wall. The view from the box looking towards the platform and Chester is spectacular, and the signalmen had a clear view of traffic movements through the station and into the motive power and freight yards, as this view shows. Norman Kneale took this view of the Up 'Day' Irish Mail, hauled by Britannia Class 4-6-2 No. **70051** *Firth of Forth*, of Crewe North shed (5A), as it took the Up Fast (centre) road through the station. The track was dead straight through the station to Bethesda Junction on a falling gradient of 1 in 660, and provided that no traffic had passed through it for a short while, the far end of the tunnel at Bethesda Junction could be clearly seen. There was a speed restriction of 50mph between Menai Bridge and Bangor, and usually steam was shut off through Belmont tunnel. Locomotives tended to roll a bit on the pointwork, after which the regulator was opened and speed picked up, and the hazy exhaust shows that the fireman had been building up his fire accordingly. The driver's headgear was not the official issue, but some Crewe North men favoured this in preference to the oilskin cap. Through the haze can be seen the carriage sidings and motive power yard on the Down side. *Norman Kneale.*

No.23. Bangor. c.1961. An unknown class 5 pulls away from the Down platform with a Holyhead train, safety valves lifting and colourless exhaust, indicating the fireman was on top of his job. In the shunting neck, a BR Standard Class 2 2-6-0 pauses momentarily before setting back into the Engineer's Yard. The Advance starter arm is prominent against the gloom of Belmont Tunnel mouth. Notice the high retaining wall on the Up side. When the station first opened, the tunnel commenced at this point, but the limited space caused shunting movements to work into the tunnel, which created numerous problems and the LNW opened out the tunnel gave sufficient space on the Down side to provide a shunting neck, as well as a Wagon Repair Shop, which was demolished after the Second World War. Notice too the usual clutter at the platform ramp, including the bilingual trespass signs.

T. Lewis.

No.24. (lower). Bangor (West End). July 1963. The summer of 1963 saw the DMU workings on the Amlwch line replaced by steam hauled push-pull trains. Here, **84001** of Llandudno Junction shed (6G) draws into Bangor's Up platform with the 12.54pm from Amlwch, worked by Bangor men, who were relieved on the platform by a Junction crew, who in turn worked forward to Llandudno Junction. This was the pattern for the Amlwch line trains for the summer season, utilising Junction Class 2 2-6-2T engines fitted for motor train working. The fitting was almost identical to that fitted on the LMS Ivatt design engines of similar appearance and the vacuum control equipment, together with the square vertical steam pipes seen alongside the smokebox, was a feature that identified the vacuum control locomotives from the rest of the class. Notice the ground disc signals with track circuit diamond indicators across the crimson band, and the line indicator arrows referring to the respective Up fast and slow lines, and the suspended Down fast starter signal. *T. Lewis.*

No.25. Bangor (West End). 1962. An unidentified Class Five, displaying a Llandudno Junction (6G) shedplate, coasts out of Belmont tunnel past No.2 signal box into the Up platform road with the first part of the 12.30pm Holyhead to Manchester Exchange train, a working signified by the headcode 1C81 A, seen hanging on the smokebox door handrail. Despite running under Class A headlamps, the train stopped at all stations between Holyhead and Llandudno Junction. After a four minute wait there it then proceeded first stop Abergele before taking the Up fast line through Rhyl to Prestatyn, its last stop before Chester. Holyhead men worked the train to the Junction, relieved by Warrington men who took over the working. B.R. Standard Class 2 2-6-0 shunts the freight yard and pulls slowly into the shunting neck on the site of the former wagon repair shop. The Down advance starter is cleared for a working from the station to Menai Bridge. Note the high retaining wall on the Up side, which was built when the tunnel was opened out to aid shunting operations in the yard which had necessitated working into the tunnel for some distance. *Norman Kneale.*

No.26. Bangor (West End). c.1963. Britannia Class 4-6-2 No.**70027** *Rising Star* of Holyhead shed (6J), passes No.2. signal box taking the Up fast line through the centre roads with a Class A passenger working, the 1.15pm to Euston (1A44) which was first stop Crewe. The train was mostly B.R. Standard Mark 1 stock, although the second coach is ex LNER steel stock, identified by the oval toilet windows at each end. Note the protecting Home signal arm, which despite being "off" is nearly horizontal, a defect which was a common cause of complaint for crews working towards Chester, and which, despite regular attention by the S.& T. staff, never seemed to be pulled off to the full distance of travel. The signalman is checking the train as it passes, his head just visible in the centre window of the cabin, whilst a colleague sits on the top step with his thermos flask prominent, enjoying the sun and the spectacle. *T. Lewis.*

No.27. **Bangor. June 1964.** Stanier Class 4 2-6-4T No.**42478** sporting a hand-painted '6H' shed code on the smoke box door pulls away from the Down Loop platform with a four coach working of B.R. Mark I coaching stock bound for Caernarfon and Afonwen. Black smoke was not normal on such workings, and judging by the grin on the fireman's face, standing behind his driver, the black smoke was for effect, and not out of necessity, and there was no desperate shortage of heat in the firebox. *Norman Kneale.*

No.28.Bangor. c.1963. Two class five 4-6-0 locomotives on a Class 'B' working might seem extravagant, as No.**44711** of 6J (Holyhead) pilots an unidentified classmate from the Down Loop platform. However the horse-boxes behind the train engine might have placed the train load over the limit, and justifying the pilot, or possibly the pilot locomotive was returning to its home depot and was attached to avoid unnecessary line occupation. *Norman Kneale.*

No.29 Bangor (Up Goods Loop). January 1965. The daily 12.00 mid-day 'Horse & Carriage' empty stock working from Holyhead to Willesden pulled into the Up Passenger Loop at Bangor at 12.41pm, where it waited for twenty seven minutes whilst stock to be worked forward was attached. This usually comprised empty vans used for mail traffic and to avoid delaying the working, the Up Side station pilot assembled these vehicles during the morning. Here Class 4 4-6-0 No.**75009** performs this task on a bitterly cold morning. Since the branch line traffic to Afonwen and Amlwch ceased, the platform was little used, and eventually was taken out of use altogether. Now it is part of a one-way traffic flow for cars departing from the car park. *Norman Kneale.*

No.30. Bangor (Up Goods Loop). 1965. Class 5 4-6-0 No.**45249** sporting an Edge Hill (8A) Liverpool shed plate draws a rake of vans forward from the Up Goods Loop line. There was considerable mail traffic to Bangor even at this time, with many overnight and early morning mails and parcels trains terminating here. After the closure of the branch lines, this traffic was worked forward by road, and vans which had previously been attached to the branch line trains now terminated here, and several were worked away on the Empty Stock working to Willesden, previously mentioned. *B.A. Wynne.*

No.31. Bangor. c.1964. This panoramic view of the platform and shed roads, taken from the site of the former Wagon Repair Shop and looking towards Chester gives some idea of the cramped conditions. The abundance of motive power was normal for a summer Saturday. A Fairburn Class 4 2-6-4T working as station passenger shunt locomotive stands on the Up platform line, presumably having attached stock to the back of a Chester train. On the Down Fast line, a Britannia Class 4-6-2 gets the signal for the centre road hauling the 11.45am Class C train bound for Holyhead. Just visible, but hidden behind the bracket signal can be seen the corner of an Ivatt Class 2 2-6-2T whilst the 8.30am Manchester to Bangor stands in the Down Passenger Loop. Another Britannia pacific is standing on the turntable road. *Norman Kneale.*

No.32. Bangor (Down Side). 2nd August 1966. Class 5 4-6-0 No.**45132** of Shrewsbury (6D) shed stands at the Down Loop platform with a three coach Class A working for Holyhead. By the date of this photograph, locomotives could find itself utilised on workings other than their official diagram and although Shrewsbury engines did not normally work to Bangor they worked into Crewe and Chester on a regular basis and could have been commandeered at short notice. On the Up passenger loop a DMU stands in the shade of the passenger and goods overbridge connecting the platforms with the booking office and station forecourt. Most of the local workings were entrusted to the DMU's and steam hauled stock was becoming rare. *B.A. Wynne.*

No.33. Bangor (Up Fast Line). 1965. Class 5 4-6-0 No.**45247** of Holyhead (6J) shed in grimy condition makes its way towards Bangor tunnel through the Up centre road, carrying Class 'K' headlamps The track has been newly relaid, and the ballast is still uneven. Behind the loco can be seen the original Thompson building, constructed for the opening of the Chester & Holyhead line. The platform is deserted although some barrow loads of mail bags are visible behind the tender, behind which can be seen a DMU in No.1 platform. *Norman Kneale.*

No.34. Bangor (Down Platform). c.1964. Royal Scot Class 4-6-0 No.**46152** *The King's Dragoon Guardsman* of Holyhead (6J) shed propels stock through the station on the Down Fast line towards Belmont tunnel and past a deserted platform 3. The reason for this movement is not known, but not unique and may be that both Up platforms were occupied at the time. The Up Fast starter signal is off and the stock will be worked into the tunnel when it will be being repositioned to take up a subsequent working once a platform road became vacant. Whatever the reason, the train was incomplete, as no tail lamp can be seen! *B.A. Wynne.*

No.35 Bangor (Motive Power Depot). 1947. Views of the Motive Power depot are not uncommon, but drifting smoke usually obscured the site and meant clear pictures were not always possible. Most photographers merely passed through, but residents or those based at the shed had the opportunity to pick their moment. Straddling the west end was a footbridge linking the Down platform with the District Engineer's Yard which provided a fine vantage point. In late 1947, the Locomotive Shed Master decided to photograph his domain in LMS days and this is the result. There is the usual activity in the Down Platform loop, with five coaches standing at the platform, with an LNW design loco hidden behind non corridor stock on the carriage siding line. In the yard Stanier 2-6-2T No.**134** takes water at the yard crane, with overspill discharging off the tank top. Notice the small hut with the telephone bell prominent. This was the 'gonging off' disk, where trainmen notified No.2. signal box that they were ready to enter traffic. There is the usual assortment LNWR design locomotives on roads 2 to 6. Probably the more modern residents were out at work. Coaching stock was parked on the two straight roads between the Motive Power yard and the Goods Shed. The coal stage can be seen alongside the shed in the distance, with its water tank level with the shed roof whilst the turntable road ran parallel to the carriage siding before ending in the 60ft turntable and pit behind the coal stage and overlooking Caernarvon Road. *J.M. Dunn.*

Motive Power

Buildings

A Motive Power department was established at Bangor with the commencement of services, and survived until 1965. Initially it was the principal shed on the North Wales coast, but under successive reorganisation schemes, its role diminished over the years. Under the 1936 Motive Power Reorganisation it became a garage shed under Llandudno Junction. The department suffered from its cramped location, and never possessed a mechanical coaling or ash disposal plant. Engines were coaled manually, and ash loaded by hand from the pits and the yard floor into wagons also by hand. A 36ft diameter turntable had been provided in 1852 but in 1859 was enlarged to 40ft diameter. It was relocated and replaced in 1884 by a 42ft diameter table when the new shed was opened, and by 1910 was replaced by a 60ft well mounted table supplied by Ransome & Rapier of Ipswich. The turntable was located at the extreme eastern edge of the shed area, hemmed in between the coal stage and the carriage sidings. It overlooked Caernarvon Road, and there was no margin of error for overshooting the turntable. A Britannia Class pacific could just be fitted on the table, and these locomotives overhung the retaining wall and the public road whilst being turned, which causing consternation to

the public who observed a locomotive projecting over the main road.

A few Official Memoranda on headed paper from the office of the Chief Locomotive Running Superintendent F. W. Dingley, at Crewe, have survived. These include one concerning the proposed new offices reported as under construction in a minute dated 16th June. Memo No.MP/29506.W dated 9th December 1920 advises the Shed Master, Mr Bostock, that agreement had been reached to provide a Bosh (a caustic soda cleaning bath) at Bangor, and requested sketches of location and enquired of the size required. Another memo, dated 10th February 1921 enquired what saving would be effected by the provision of a telephone change-over switch at the shed, followed up eight days later with another memo agreeing to provide the switch. On a different topic, Memo dated 15th February 1921 headed General position of steam sheds, 1/12/21'. Mr Dingleys office remarked that 'Bangor shed will hold 20 engines and stabling room for 15 engines outside'. Clarification on the size of engines referred to is requested. A hand-written note has been added, stating this refers to 20 small and 13 large engines. Also added is in the case of

Carnarvon the engines stationed there at present are 8 small and 3 large.

Locomotives

The earliest record of locomotives allocated was abstracted by Mr C. Williams, the well-known LNWR historian, from the Crewe records at the behest of J.M. Dunn. Accommodation at Bangor shed in 1859 and 1866 was for 12 engines. By 1873 Bangor had an allocation of 37 engines. A typewritten copy of Minute No.83 of the Locomotive & Engine Committee, dated 12th October 1864 gives the entry for Bangor as follows:

PASSENGER		GOODS		SHUNTING	BALLAST
Main Line	Branch	Main Line	Branch		
9	7	6	-	3	3

J.M. Dunn commented in a handwritten notebook that in 1908, 2-4-0, 4ft 6ins engines Nos. 1000 and 1001 were stationed at Bangor for working the Red Wharf Bay and Bethesda branches, and added that both gave a lot of trouble with hot trailing axleboxes.

A memo addressed to Mr Nevitt, Bangor, from C.J. Bowen Cooke, Chief Mechanical Engineer, Crewe, dated 29th June 1917 and headed Cambrian Companys Engines loaned to the L&NW Co. On the reverse side is a handwritten note in pencil stating Engine 73 6-wheeled coupled goods received on 27/6/17 put to work 28/6/17. Engine 85 4-wheeled coupled Pass. engine received 28/6/17 put to work 29/6/17. Engine 47 4-wheeled coupled engine received 29/6/17 put to work 29/6/17, signed A. Nevitt, and dated 30/6/17.

An interesting letter amongst J.M. Dunn's papers was from the Assistant Branch Manager of Shell-Mex and B.P. Ltd., dated 3rd March 1934, and addressed to J. T. King, District Locomotive Superintendent, Llandudno Junction, seeking an interview with Mr King about the proposed introduction of two oil-fired high pressure steam Sentinel rail coaches at Bangor. Extensive research has failed to produce any information on which steam rail car was contemplated, and more interestingly, for which lines they were intended.

Bangor Engine Allocations

SEPTEMBER 1926.
LNWR Precedent Class 1P 2-4-0
Nos.   5015 *Gladiator*, 5067 *Lowther*.
LNWR Renown Class 2P 4-4-0
No.   5161 *Sultan*.
LNWR Precursor Class 3P 4-4-0
No.   5304 *Greyhound*.
LNWR Geo V Class 2P 4-4-0
No.   5322 *F. S. P. Wolferstan*.
LNWR Experiment Class 3P 4-6-0
Nos.   5475 *Ivanhoe*, 5487 *Combermere*, 5529 *Berenice*.

September 1926 (continued)
LNWR Claughton Class 5P 4-6-0
Nos.   5915 *Rupert Guinness*, 5920 *George Macpherson*, 5930 *G. R. Jebb*.
LNWR 4ft 6ins. Class 1P 2-4-2T
Nos.   6569, 6583.
LNWR 5ft 6ins. Class 1P 2-4-2T
Nos.   6702, 6717, 6726.
LNWR Class 1F 0-6-2T
Nos.   7557, 7558, 7560, 7580, 7651, 7693, 7695, 7696, 7739. 7749, 7751, 7756, 7837, 7841.
LNWR Class Special DX Class 0-6-0
Nos.   8014, 8055,
LNWR 17" Coal Engines 0-6-0
No.   8249.
LNWR Cauliflower Class 2F 0-6-0
Nos.   8331, 8463, 8511, 8545, 8577.
LNWR Class (G) 4F 0-8-0
No.   9124.
LNWR Class (F) 3F 2-8-0 4-cyl compound.
No.   9611.
G.C.R. Robinson (ex W.D.) 2-8-0
No.   9645.

JULY 1929.
PASSENGER ENGINES
Renown Class:Nos.5152. *King Arthur*, 5157.*Jubilee*.
Geo.V Class:	Nos.	5371. *Moorhen*, 5372.*Wild Duck*, 5373. *Ptarmigan*.
Experiment Class:	Nos.	5545. *Leicestershire*, 5546. *Middlesex*.
Claughton Class:	Nos.	6026, 6027, 6028.
4' 6" Motor:	Nos.	6578, 6579.
5' 6" S.T.	Nos.	6633, 6635, 6636, 6637, 6748.
5' 6" Superh. S.T.	Nos.	6963, 6964, 6965.

FREIGHT ENGINES
M. M. Class	Nos.	9644, 9645, 9646, 9647, 9649.
Std Freight 0-6-0	Nos.	4146, 4147, 4148.
S.T.C. (Motor)	Nos.	7557, 7654, 7679, 7680.
S.T.C.	Nos.	7795, 7796, 7797, 7799, 7801, 7802, 7803, 7805.
Small Coal	Nos.	8158, 8159.
18" Goods.	Nos.	8354, 8355, 8370, 8537, 8538, 8539, 8540, 8541, 8542.
19" Goods.	Nos.	8779, 8780, 8781.

OCTOBER 1938
Class 3 2-6-2T Parallel boiler
Nos.   2, 12, 48, 51, 52, 55, 70, 101.
Class 3 2-6-2T Taper boiler.
Nos.   101, 207.
Class 4F 0-6-0
Nos.   4075, 4121, 4305, 4340, 4375, 4487.
Class 5 4-6-0.
Nos.   5070, 5317, 5318, 5346.
5' 6" 2-4-2T Vacuum Control.

October 1938 (continued)
Nos. **6681, 6683, 6703, 6710.**
Coal engine 0-6-0
No. **8158.**
18" 0-6-0
Nos. **8485, 8618, 8392.**
0-6-0. ex L.& Y.
Nos. **12214, 12605.**
Precursor Class 4-4-0
No. **25277.** *Oberon.*
Geo.V. Class 4-4-0
No. **25374.** *Vanguard.*
0-6-2T S.T.C.
Nos. **27596, 27604, 27654, 27678, 7728, 7729, 7764, 7812.**

SEPTEMBER 1944.
Class 3 PT 2-6-2 Taper Boiler.
Nos. **72, 73, 123, 133, 134, 137.**
Class 2P 4-4-0
Nos. **495, 671.**
Class 4P 4-4-0
No. **1093.**
Class 5F 2-6-0
Nos. **2948, 2951, 2984.**
Class 4F 0-6-0
Nos. **4305, 4445.**
Class 1PT 5'6" 2-4-2T
Nos. **6643, 6645, 6669, 6713, 6755.**
Class 1PT 5'6" 2-4-2T Vacuum Control.
Nos. **6710, 6725.**
Class 2PT 0-6-2T 18" S.T.
No. **6926.**
Class 2FT 0-6-2T S.T.C.
Nos. **7705, 7721, 7808, 7812, 27561, 27619, 27654.**
Class 2FT 0-6-2T S.T.C. Vacuum Control
Nos. **7710, 27602, 27603, 27604, 7822.**
Class 3F ex L.& Y. 0-6-0
Nos. **12176, 12230, 12407.**
Class 2F 0-6-0 18".
Nos. **28392, 28404, 28513, 28553, 28618.**

JUNE 1952
Class 3MTT 2-6-2T Taper Boiler.
No. **40132.**
Class 2MTT 2-6-2T
Nos. **41200, 41230, 41232, 41233, 41239.**
Class 2MTT 2-6-2T Vacuum Control
Nos. **41223, 41287, 41324.**
Class 4MTT 2-6-4T
Nos. **42156, 42157, 42234, 42258, 42259, 42260, 42261, 42455, 42460, 42588, 42617, 42628, 42663, 42670.**
Class 4F 0-6-0
Nos. **44305, 44445.**
Class 5 4-6-0
Nos. **44913, 45144, 45417.**

June 1952 (continued)
Class 1PT 5'6" 2-4-2T
Nos. **46604, 46701.**
Class 3F 0-6-0 L.& Y.
Nos. **52119, 52162, 12269, 52230.**
Class 2F 0-6-0 18"
Nos. **58375, 28589.**
Class 2FT 0-6-2T S.T.C.
No. **58903.**

13th JUNE 1960
Class 3MTT 2-6-2T
Nos. **40071, 40076, 40078, 40132, 40136.**
Class 2MTT 2-6-2T
Nos. **41200, 41230, 41233, 41234, 41237, 41239, 41244.**
Class 4MTT 2-6-4T
Nos. **42074, 42075, 42076, 42247, 42270, 42416, 42487, 42489, 42544, 42562, 42567, 42601, 42674.**
Class 5MT 4-6-0
Nos. **44913, 45144, 45225, 45247, 45302, 45345, 45417.**
Class 3F 0-6-0T
Nos. **47267, 47511.**
Class 2MT 2-6-0
Nos. **78058, 78059.**

Motive Power Department Staff

The Staff Allocation at Bangor on 4th September 1944 was as follows:

FOOTPLATE STAFF
Drivers	50	
Drivers over 65 years	2	
Passed Firemen	21	
Firemen	31	
Firemen ex Drivers over 65 years	1	
Passed Cleaners	28	Total 133
GOODS GUARDS	22	Total 22

SHED STAFF
Ashfillers	1	
Barboys	2	
Callers-Up (male)	2	
Callers-Up (female)	1	
Chargeman Cleaner	1	
Coalmen	4	
Firedroppers	4	
Foremans Assistant	1	
Labourers (Female)	5	
Shed Labourers (Male)	8	
Steam Raisers	2	
Stores Issuers	3	
Tube Cleaners	4	Total 38

REPAIRED ENGINES STAFF
Boilersmith	1
Leading Fitter	1
Fitter Grade 1.	5
Fitter Grade 3.	1
Fitters Mates	2

REPAIRED ENGINES STAFF (continued)

Fitters Mate (Female)	1			
Tubers	1			
Brick-arch-man	1	Total	13	

SALARIED STAFF

Running Shed Foreman	1			
Running Shift Foreman	1			
Clerks Male Adult	2			
Clerks Female Adult	2	Total	6	

Total Number of Motive Power Department Staff   212

ENGINEMEN

Details of the numbers of men employed on the footplate staff at Bangor prior to the arrival of J.M. Dunn are practically non-existent, although one or two personal records have survived, and are worth recording here. They were abstracted from the Staff Record of LNWR Enginemen by Mr Dunn.

James McKie.   Born 12th May 1829.

Engaged	June	1848.		
Appointed Cleaner	June	1848		
Fireman	July	1853		
Engineman	March	1858	Rate	7/-d per day
	July	1887		6/6d
	Oct.	1889		7/-

Retired owing to old age. 8th March 1901

Remarks:

15th March 1891	Suspended 7 days for irregularity in working Bethesda Branch Train Staff.
18th Sept. 1895	Fined 10/- for causing Engine No.417 to leave the rails at Bethesda Junction.

Joseph Williams. Born 7th July 1828.

Engaged	June	1850		
Appointed Cleaner	June	1850		
Fireman	Dec.	1850		
Engineman	Oct.	1865	Rate	7/-d per day
	July	1882		6/6d
	Oct.	1889		7/-d

Died 28th November 1896.

Robert Prydderch.   Born 12th March 1847.

Engaged	June	1863		
Appointed Fireman	Oct.	1871		
Engineman	Oct.	1874	Rate	6/6d per day
	March	1883		7/- d
Fireman	Oct.	1886		4/- d
Engineman	July	1887		6/6d
	Oct.	1889		6/6d
	May	1891		7/6d
	May	1896		7/- d

Died 28th March 1903.

Remarks:

28th Sept. 1886	Reduced to Firing for 6 months. Mr. Whales letter 29:9:86

15th January 1891	Fined 5/-d for neglecting to fill tank before leaving shed thus causing delay. 10:12:90.
20th July 1892	Suspended 7 days for causing mishap at Bangor.
5th June 1895	Suspended 2 days for missing train after being called.
16th January 1896	Fined 2/6d for not getting up when called at Crewe Lodging House 4:1:96
20th Dec. 1900	No details. For causing damage to chimney of Engine No.3446, 13th December 1900.

William Roberts. Born 21st July 1849.

Engaged	Nov.	1869.		
Appointed Cleaner	Nov.	1869		
Fireman	July	1871		
Turner	July	1877		
Engineman	July	1878	Rate	5/-d per day
	April	1882		6/6d
	April	1885		7/-d
	Oct.	1889		7/6d

Died 26th January 1905.

Remarks:

30th May 1895	Fined 7/-d for overshooting platform at Caernarvon.
18th Nov. 1897	Suspended 1 day for coming late on duty.
20th May 1898	Suspended 1 day for smoke nuisance etc. at Llandudno Junction.
2nd August 1899	Suspended 1 day for causing mishap at Lime Street station.
28th February 1900	Suspended 1 day for causing mishap at Crewe South Shed 15th February 1900.
1st December 1903	Suspended 1 day for smoke nuisance at Penmaenmawr.

William Samuel Williams.   D. of B. not known.

Details of the railway career of Will Sam, as he was known, are not recorded, other than he progressed through the normal line of promotion and was an Engineman about the turn of the century. He was a fiery character and was sacked for fighting a guard. He then set up as an "out porter", taking commercial travellers skips from shop to shop until with the advent of the motor car, this business went out.

He had a number of sons, all of whom carried the title "Will Sam". Two were drivers at Bangor, and were known as Will (Will Sam) and Bob (Will Sam). It is believed that both brothers were still on the footplate in September 1944.

Below is a list of all Motive Power staff for June 1952, extracted from J.M. Dunns notebooks, but excluding Office Staff. It is believed to be complete and correct. The list is compiled in order of seniority and apologies are tendered if there are any omissions. Figures in brackets are pay numbers.

DRIVERS.

(3) P. Tharme; (5) D. Williams; (7) W. Williams; (8) R.E. Williams; (10) A.O. Williams; (11) G.L. Jones; (12) P. Williams; (13) A.W. Williams; (14) W.R.J. Read; (16) H. Jones; (17) W.H.

DRIVERS (continued)

Davies; (18) W. Jones; (19) E. Owens; (20) T. Williams; (21) O. Edwards; (22) G. Jones; (23) W. Smith; (24) T. Parry; (25) V.N.B. Edwards; (26) R.I. Roberts; (27) R.J. Williams; (28) W.I. Roberts; (29) A.V. Williams; (31) R.R. Hughes; (32) H.J. Davies; (33) G. Williams; (34) H. Owen; (35) R. Thomas; (36) W. Davies; (37) H. Roberts; (38) H. Caulfield; (39) J. Hughes; (40) W. Roberts; (41) W.E. Jones; (42) E. Davies; (43) Ll. Griffiths; (44) D.J. Jones; (45) R. Jones; (46) H. Hughes; (47) A. Jones; (48) D. Roberts; (49) W. Jones; (50) H.S. Roberts; (52) E. Roberts; (53) W.J. Graham; (54) J.J. Roberts; (58) W. Jones; (59) W.L. Ellis; (60) R.E. Davies; (61) R.E. Price; (62) I.S. Kelly; (63) F.W. Morgan; (64) W.S. Dean; (65) C. Ellis.

PASSED FIREMEN.
(66) M. Edwards; (67) A.R. Leyshon; (68) J.N. Davies; (69) W.A. Griffiths; (70) D.L. Jones; (71) A.O. Hughes; (72) J.E. Jones; (73) G. Williams; (74) E. Lynn; (76) O.G. Roberts; (77) S.V. Jones; (78) W.J. Williams; (79) W.N. Jones; (80) J.M. Williams; (81) W.E. Humphreys; (83) O.E. Hughes.

FIREMEN.
(84) F.S. Hughes; (85) O.T. Evans; (86) E.O. Hughes; (87) R. Edwards; (89) D. Humphreys; (90) D.L. Owen; (91) J. Mooney; (92) W.O. Williams; (93) A.W. Hughes; (94) W.I. Roberts; (95) J.O. Williams; (96) J.I. Jones; (97) R.A. Hughes; (98) G. Davies; (99) R. Humphreys; (100) I. Williams; (101) J.R. Jones; (102) J. Williams; (103) J.T. Jones; (104) J.H. Williams; (105) R.A. Williams; ((106) J.R. Jones; (110) G. Pritchard; (111) A. Roberts; (112) H. Blain; (113) T.A. Hughes; (114) W.E. Davies; (115) L. Hughes; (116) T.J. Jones; (117) R.E. Pritchard; (119) E.G. Owen; (122) T.J. Williams.

PASSED CLEANERS.
(121) A.H. Williams; (123) G.R. Williams; (124) G.E. Williams; (125) F. Johnson; (126) E.W. Davies; (131) M.P. Jones; (133) J.R. Cropper; (134) E.O. Parry; (136) J.W. Jones; (137) C.W. Simpson; (138) D. Williams; (139) W.A. Thomas; (140) D.I. Ellis; (141) R.B. Roberts; (142) J. Herd; (143) K. Edwards; (144) W.A. Hughes; (145) E. Pritchard; (148) G.L. Hughes; (149) W.I. Williams; (151) G.H. Ellis; (153) R.D. Jones; (159) A.H. MacIntosh;

CLEANERS.
(146) J.R. Williams; (147) G.J. Hughes; (150) T.R. Owen; (152) K. Williams; (154) E.M. Williams; (155) E. Evans; (156) R.L. Roberts; (160) I.T.P. Jones; (162) J.G. Owen; (163) A. Thomas; (165) T.A. Owen; (166) J.W. Hughes; (167) R.H. Hughes; (168) L.W. Williams; (169) W. Evans; (170) R.A.L. Jones; (171) J.E. Jones; (172) A.I. Pugh; (173) R. Roberts; (174) D.Y.Williams; (175) A. Davies; (176) T.I.McAdams; (177) J.T. Roberts; (178) C. Williams; (179) H. Williams; (180) D.A. Edwards; (181) L.A. Griffiths; (182) R. Williams; (183) W.R. Owen; (184) T. Ansley; (185) L. Morris; (186) K. Anstay; (187) M.R. Evans; (188) T.G. Jones; (189) V.R. Humphreys; (190) J.W. Jones.

SHED STAFF.
(203) D.O. Pritchard - Chargehand Cleaner; (204) J.H. Wright - Coalman; (205) N. Aile - Coalman; (206) E.F. Williams - Coalman; (207) I. Thomas - Coalman; (208) J. Ansonia - Steamraiser;

SHED STAFF (continued)

(209) J.O. Jones - Steamraiser; (210) A. Jones - Steamraiser; (212) C. Williams - Firedropper; (213) A. Candwall - Toolman; (214) J.E. Wright - Firedropper; (215) J.P. Roberts - Firedropper; (216) A. Hogan - Firedropper; (218) E. Jones - Boilerwasher; (219) W.H. Roberts - Stores Issuer; (220) H. Hughes - Stores Issuer; (222) R.E. Roberts - Labourer; (224) W.R. Davies - Stores Issuer; (225) G. Williams - Stores Issuer; (227) J. Williams - Labourer; (228) H.L. Hughes - Labourer; (233) O.W. Griffiths - Coalman; (234) R.O. Roberts - Labourer; (235) G. Pritchard - Labourer; (237) R. Hughes - Barman; (242) A. Harknett - Water Plant Attendant; (243) H. Morris - Labourer; (251) H. Bargh - Labourer; (252) J.D. Taylor - Labourer; (255) J.R. Barnett - Labourer; (257) R. Williams - Labourer; (259) B. Lewis - Labourer.

REPAIRED ENGINES STAFF.
(260) C.W. Farr - Boilersmith; (261) D. Hughes - Brick-archman; (263) G. Bellis - Chargehand Fitter; (265) M. Thompson - Fitter; (266) R.C. Hughes - Fitter; (267) R.H. Owen - Fitter; (268) E. Owen - Fitter; (269) A.M. Thomas - Fitter; (270) T.O. Hughes - Fitter; (271) J.M. Morris - Fitter; (273) R.E. Roberts - Fitters Mate; (274) L. Williams - Fitters Mate; (275) H. Roberts - Fitters Mate; (276) A.J. Owen - Fitters Mate; (277) T.J. Short - Tuber.

By 1953 there were 52 sets of enginemen, and the total number of staff employed in the motive power department was 211, of which 40 were named Williams and 31 in that of Jones! This number included 20 goods guards in the compliment.

No.36 Bangor (Motive Power Yard). c.1950. Driver and fireman stand alongside LNW 0-6-2T No.**58903** at the start of their shift. These locos were much in evidence on passenger and freight work until replaced by the Ivatt Class 2MT 2-6-2T engines after the Second World War, and were a decided improvement for accessibility during preparation and disposal duties not to mention personal comfort in the cab whilst on the road. This example was equipped for motor train working, hence the two vacuum pipes prominent against the bunker.
G.H. Platt.

No.37. Bangor. Motive Power Yard. 1949. No.46604 stands awaiting time before moving off shed to run light engine to Caernarvon for the yard shunt there. It had not long come off works, having gained its new number, although the powers that be decided that the overhaul didn't justify the cost of providing a transfer on the tanks. These 5' 6" engines were much in evidence at Bangor, and until replaced by the Ivatt 2-6-2T engines were to be found on Bethesda and Amlwch branches, working push-pull 'motor' trains, hence the twin vacuum pipes. Stanier 2-6-4T No.42460 sets back on the Down Loop Platform line to pick up its stock.   *G.H. Platt.*

No.38. Bangor. Motive Power Yard. 1948. Ex. LNWR 0-6-2T No.7721 shunts the Goods Warehouse in the spring of 1948, still displaying the number and lettering of the previous owner. These tank engines were nearing the end of their active life, and generally spent their days with long periods of idleness briefly interrupted for the movement of wagons in the goods or District Engineers Yards. Passed cleaners were trained on such workings as this, generally partnered by drivers who were working out their service on undemanding duties and who had time, if not the inclination, to explain the intricacies of the machine and supervise the first attempts at keeping the steam pressure and water levels within acceptable limits. They were not the most comfortable of engines to work, and it was rumoured that F.W.Webb designed the beast for the specific purpose of skinning knuckles!   *G.H. Platt.*

No.39. Bangor. Motive Power Yard. 1950. Ex LNWR 0-6-0 No.58375 stands out of steam on No.1 shed road, coupled to another LNW 0-6-2T. Behind a Stanier 2-8-0 is being prepared for duty, the driver's oil bottle and oilcan on the front framing. Behind the 8F is No.41200, a long time resident at the shed and the first of the class.   *G.H. Platt.*

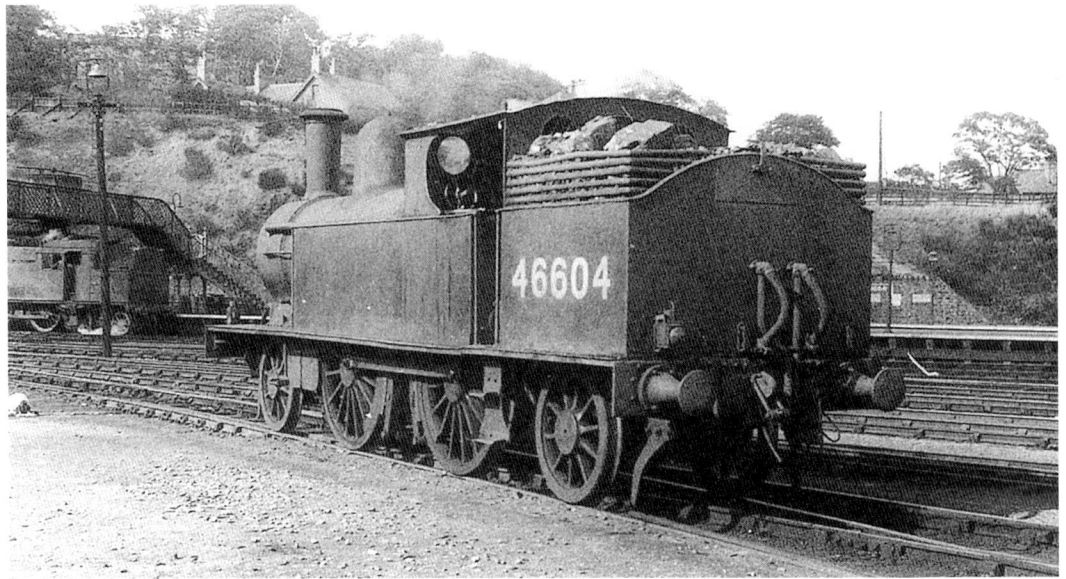

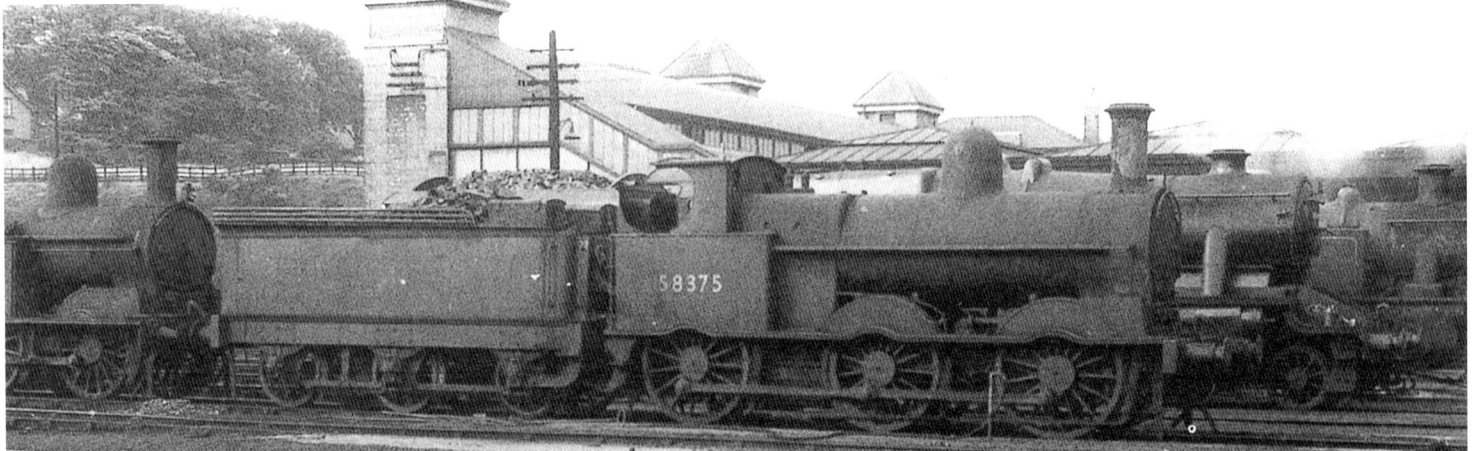

No.40. J. M. Dunn's office in 1954.   Mark Radley & Co.

It was a well-known fact that J.M. Dunn took a cynical attitude towards some of his superiors and also to those members of his staff, whatever the grade, whose performance exploited and abused their position, and this was reflected in his writings. Conversely he showed care, consideration and compassion to his staff who worked to the best of their ability, and displayed endless patience with, and gave encouragement to the younger and wilder elements who responded to his authority. He gave undivided loyalty to all his staff at Bangor, which was recognised in turn and appreciated by most of the staff.

Amongst J.M. Dunn's papers held by the author is a large scrapbook containing copies of official correspondence covering the period from 1935 up to the date of his retirement on 27th September 1958. It was Mr Dunn's main source of reference and evidence and which was frequently in demand! Whilst much of the correspondence between himself and his District or Divisional Office was routine and non-controversial, at times matters arose that were out of the ordinary, and copies of the relevant correspondence was kept and pasted up. In the back of this scrapbook are a sequence of letters, describing a chain of events which culminated in his premature retirement, which had been contrived by someone in the L.M.Region Management with that specific purpose in mind.

This commenced with the appointment of a Mr L. Lancaster to the position of Running Foreman at Bangor in March 1957. Mr Lancaster had spent twelve months in a Control Office and before that had been a fireman at Macclesfield prior to his appointment to Bangor.

The first indication of the chain of events comes in an internal memo, numbered 6H/1511 dated 14:10:57 addressed to Mr A.E. Fairhead, District Motive Power Superintendent at Chester headed:

Mr L. Lancaster - Running Foreman

'*Please note the attached letter which I have received from Mr Lancaster for forwarding to you.*

I had refrained from saying anything about Mr Lancaster in the hope that it might eventually be unnecessary for me to do so, until Mr Froud asked a question to which, unfortunately, I had to give an unpleasant answer.

I regret to say that Mr Lancaster has a tactless and unfortunate manner which antagonises all members of staff. I am repeatedly having complaints about the way in which he speaks to men and I had three last week, each of the men concerned being among the best members of staff and individuals who have never given trouble, I cannot afford to have them upset.

The esteem in which Mr Lancaster is held is such that he was publicly hanged in effigy from the top of the jib of the diesel crane in full view of passers-by on the Caernarvon Road when I was on holiday. I believe he had to climb the jib himself after it had been on exhibition 24 hours. He has decided views of his own which he follows obstinately and he will take no guidance from either example or precept. He is obviously of the opinion that he "knows it all" and will listen to advice from no one. He always argues the point and tries to have the last word.

I am sorry to say that he holds a position of authority without having the least idea of those good manners which are such an essential accomplishment in one who has to handle men.

Mr Lancaster came here on March 4th and was given a cordial reception which was followed by a week on each shift, plus another week with me so that I could show him how to handle staff to the best advantage. Everything appertaining to the duties of a Running Foreman were explained to him with the promise of wider tuition concerning all phases of Running Shed work once he had settled down. When he took over the duties of Running Foreman I arranged for him to have assistance for the first few week-ends and he thanked me for all this by telling me that I had given him a "raw deal". Further, on the occasion of the land slide at Menai Bridge when it was necessary to call out staff specially on a Sunday morning, he tried his arrogance on me by indignantly asking why he had not been sent for.

I soon found out that Mr Lancaster had neither the manners nor the intelligence to appreciate the difference in our positions (in regard to rank, if not in classification) ages, or experience and I have had, after six months endeavour to mould him by ordinary rational means, to give this up and to speak to him in a manner which he has at last understood, hence his letter to you which I enclose.

I told Mr Lancaster on Friday that I was not going to have my staff bullied and that the best thing he could do was to apply for a transfer as after the way he has antagonised all sections of the staff he would do no good at Bangor.

I deeply regret both having to write such a letter and to trouble you with it but Mr Lancaster has now left me no alternative.'

A month later, the Secretary of the Staff Side of the Local Departmental Committee, D. Humphreys, formally wrote to Mr Dunn, requesting an L.D.C. meeting with Mr Fairhead on consultation level following a branch meeting held on 10th November. The subject for discussion was the request for the removal from Bangor of R.S.F. L. Lancaster. The letter states that backing from all grades including shed staff on this matter was 100%.

A meeting was held on 21st November at which the D.M.P.S. attended, and a letter received which stated that Mr Fairhead had spoken to Mr Lancaster and he hoped there would be an improvement in the working relationship.

Things did not improve, and Mr Dunn wrote once more to Mr Fairhead on 9th January 1958, pointing out that matters had only changed for the worse, and requesting his removal from office. Another letter followed on 5th February, when Mr Dunn pointed out that Mr Lancaster was undermining his authority. It transpired that Mr Lancaster had taken matters into his own hands, and was by-passing Mr Dunn, dealing directly with the District M.P.S.

By 31st March, matters had deteriorated so much that Mr Dunn wrote to the Divisional Motive Power Superintendent at Crewe as follows:

I *must apologise for the breach of etiquette in writing to you direct instead of through Mr Fairhead but he is aware of what I am doing and I am sending him copies of this letter and enclosures.*

It is not necessary for me to enlarge upon the matter as the enclosed copies of letters I have forwarded to Chester speak for themselves and you will see from them that my position here is, to put it mildly, exceedingly difficult.

Will you kindly take some action in the matter.

Apparently nothing happened, and Mr Dunn wrote to Mr Fairhead on 3rd April enclosing copies of letters sent to Mr E.H. Baker and the Line Traffic Officer (Motive Power) Crewe, about the intolerable situation at Bangor.

There then follows a gap in the correspondence until a very distressed letter from Mr Dunn to Mr Fairhead, dated 30th July 1958 appears. The letter suggests conspiracy in high places and states that Mr Lancaster was now dealing direct with Chester at a level that was clearly above his rank and had totally undermined Mr Dunn's authority at Bangor. He concluded by asking for five days leave of absence over the busiest week-end of the year.

The five days were spent reviewing his situation and in fact Mr Dunn consulted with several trusted friends before reaching a decision. Once this was decided, he lost no time in implementing it, and on return to work, tendered his resignation to take effect from 30th September 1958. A letter in the scrapbook from the Internal Relations Officer at Euston House and dated 20th August 1958 comments that the Officer had received information of his impending retirement and ...... wanted to make some reference to his interests and activities in the LMR magazine. News travelled fast! Mr Dunn obliged, and spent the next few weeks in comparative peace. His final Personal Report to the District Motive Power Superintendent at Chester contains no reference to Mr Lancaster, but the final paragraph contains one final gem which summarises his feelings towards his employers. I quote:

I retire from the service of the British Transport Commission after duty today and so this is my last Personal Report. I should have completed 45 years service on the 11th November next but as a personal contribution to the efforts to restore

the British Transport Commission to financial stability I decided to retire before I was due to receive a presentation time-piece.!

That there had been a conspiracy to remove him from office is not in any doubt. Throughout his working life Max Dunn had been a thorn in the flesh of some of his superiors on the LMS and British Railways. He had the knack of finding the weaknesses of his superiors, particularly if there was some buck-passing or cover-up taking place and exposing them publicly. His feelings towards Trades Unions, Freemasons and other bodies was well known, and having crossed their paths early in his working life, continued to do so until he retired. Perhaps the seeds of his final downfall had its origins in 1947 when he was confronted by J.W. Watkins, LMS Divisional Operating Manager, and J.S. Elliot, the Motive Power Assistant, when he was summoned to Crewe and 'hauled over the coals' for alleged autocratic behaviour towards his staff. The background to this can be found in his autobiography '*Reflections on a Railway Career*' pages 137-8. The injustice of this onslaught prompted JMD to prepare a catalogue of events and happenings from the day he took over at Bangor. This ran to 28 sides and on completion was placed before a Commissioner of Oaths and a Statutory Declaration made as to its truth. Copies were then sent to Messrs Watkin and Colonel Rudgard, Superintendent of Motive Power at Euston. The author also has a copy of this amazing document. The outcome was that the Colonel eventually met up with Mr Dunn, and expressed confidence in his abilities, which was the official way of smoothing things over. However despite promises of promotion, these never materialised, and he remained at Bangor until he retired. In fact the incident was never forgotten, and despite the fact that Bangor shed was a model of efficiency, there were a few individuals who brooded on the fact that Max Dunn had not been dismissed, and nurtured him a grudge. In fairness, Mr Whitehead, District Motive Power Superintendent at Chester, and his predecessor, Mr H. Rihll, were both very supportive of the hard work done at Bangor, the obvious improvements in morale and efficiency and the stand taken, but were themselves out-ranked and therefore powerless to intervene when the Lancaster dispute erupted. It is interesting to note that six months after his retirement, L. Lancaster disappeared abruptly from Bangor, and his subsequent movements have not been traced.

No.41. Bangor (Down Platform).29th June 1954. Collett 0-6-0 No.**3202** worked the first Western Region Land Cruise train from Pwllheli, which worked the circuit in the reverse direction, seen here at Bangor, the first time a GWR engine had visited the station, worked by Pwllheli men with an LM pilotman   *J.M. Dunn.*

No.42. Bangor. Motive Power Yard. May 1951. Most of the residents of Bangor shed were out in service on the day this photograph was taken, with pre-group locomotives outnumbering their more modern counterparts. The identity of the LNW engine in the foreground is obscured by the acute angle of the photograph, whilst 0-6-2T No.**58903** stands in front of a Stanier Class 8F 2-8-0 on No.1 road. L.& Y. 0-6-0 No.**52119** stands in front of Fowler 0-6-0 No.**44445**.

D. Chaplin.

No.43. Bangor. Motive Power Yard. 1947. Fairburn 2-6-4T No.**2260** was one of a batch of four that arrived at Bangor on 13th January 1947 from Crewe North, where they had been placed on entering traffic in week ending 7th December 1946. These Class 4 tanks replaced Class 3 2-6-2T engines which moved to Llandudno Junction. The four spent eight years at Bangor working Afonwen and Llandudno Junction turns before being transferred to Greenock in early 1954, in exchange for four Fowler engines of the same configuration. *G.H. Platt.*

No.44. Bangor. Motive Power Yard. 1955. Taken during the National Strike and shows the yard, sidings and platform roads full. A single plume of smoke rises from a solitary class 5 that worked a service to Crewe and back manned by a volunteer crew who did not participate in the industrial action. *J.M. Dunn.*

No.45. Bangor. 1960. This view shows the station complex in the summer of 1960, and the absence of drifting smoke shows the west end of the station very clearly. Steam escaping from safety valves betray the presence of a locomotive on the coal stage road, and another on the shed roads. The Up Platform Loop starter is pulled off and another column of smoke indicates that something is moving slowly towards Bangor tunnel.
G.H. Platt.

No.46. Bangor. Motive Power Yard. 1947. LNWR passenger engines were becoming increasingly thin on the ground by 1947. Here what turned out to be the last survivor of the once numerous 'Precursor' Class locomotive, No.**25297** *Sirocco* stands in the yard awaiting its next turn of duty. This locomotive was allocated to Llandudno Junction shed (7A) and worked local passenger turns between Chester and Holyhead. It appears in good physical shape, and is presentably clean, but cessation of hostilities, which had given surviving members of the class a brief reprieve, meant that it would soon be replaced by one of the ubiquitous class 5 4-6-0 mixed traffic locomotives. *G.H. Platt.*

No.47. Bangor. Down platform. 1947. LNWR 5ft 6ins. No.**6710,** a member of the 1P Class 2-4-2T stands at the Down platform after working the push-pull 'motor' train from Caernarfon, and would shortly continue to Bethesda, hence it standing in the Down platform. Notice the short lived style of lettering and numbering on the tank and bunker sides, that was introduced in 1937 but was superceded after a year.
G.H. Platt.

No.48. Bangor. May 1948. Ex LNWR 0-6-2T No.**6899** was a long term resident of Bangor shed, as were several members of the class, and worked over most of the branch lines until superceded by the Ivatt 2-6-2T after the war. This engine then undertook more lowly duties, acting as station and Permanent Way Yard shunt, and for several months in 1950 travelled daily to act as Caernarfon Yard Shunt. It transferred away to Monument Lane in December 1951, still carrying its LMS initials and numbers. *G.H. Platt.*

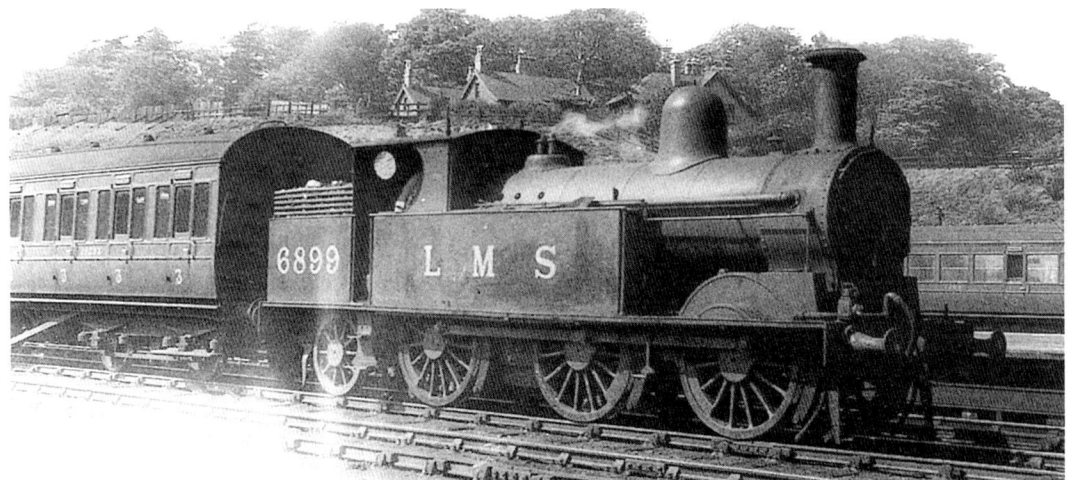

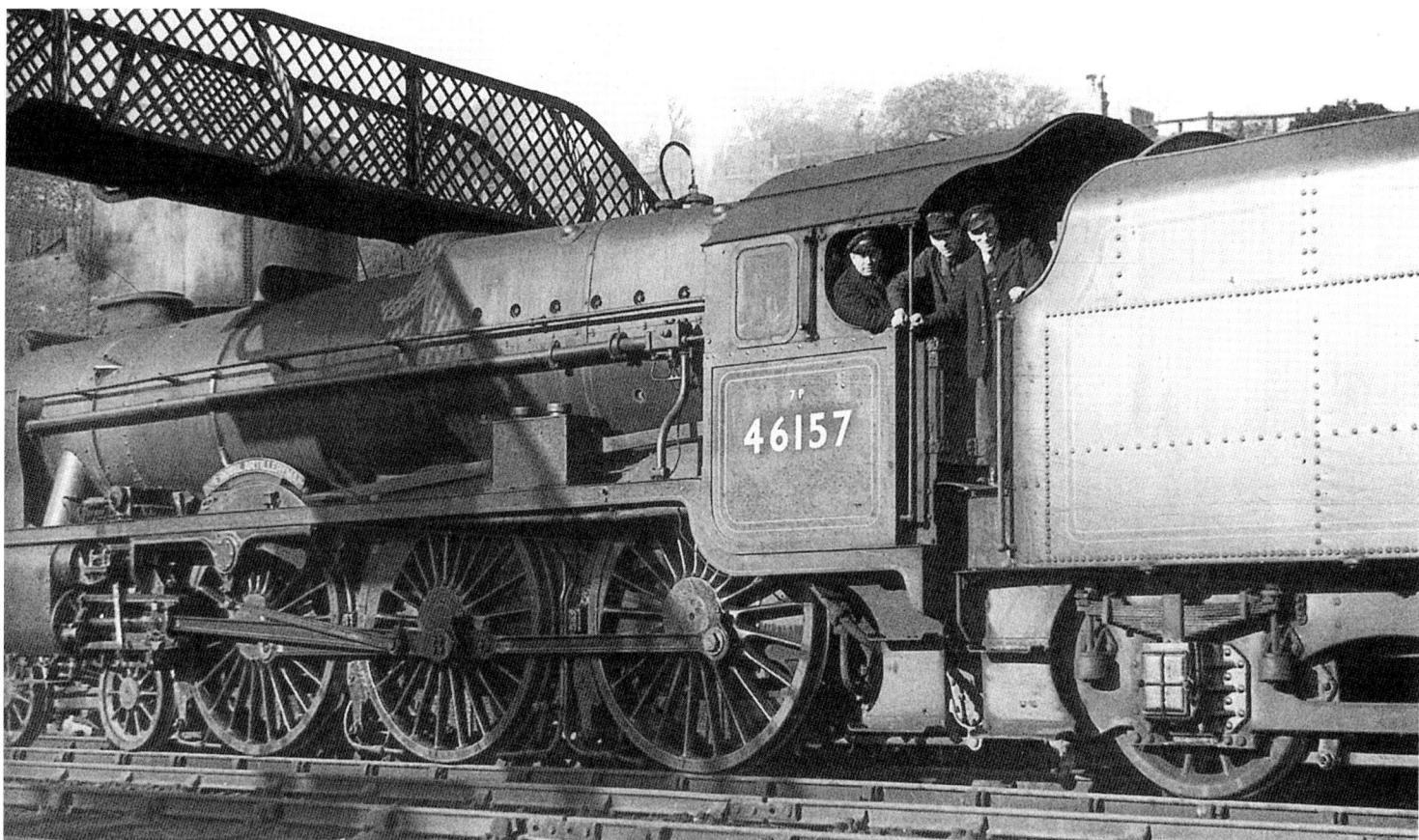

No.49. Bangor (Down Passenger Loop Platform). 15th November 1952. Rebuilt Royal Scot Class 4-6-0 No.**46157** T*he Royal Artilleryman* stands on the Down side loop, having worked the 9.20am from Crewe to Holyhead. The loco detached from the train and transferred a van onto the 12.20pm Afonwen working which worked from platform 4. Once this move was completed, the loco resumed its place at the head of the stock and continued to Holyhead at 12.03pm. This was a regular movement, and a shunter was on hand to effect the coupling and uncoupling, which had to be completed within eleven minutes. The photographer offered some advice, which the traincrew rejected politely, but nevertheless they posed for the photograph and demanded prints in due course.   *W.G. Rear.*

No.50. Bangor Motive Power Yard. c.1964. Class 5 4-6-0 No.**45345** of Bangor (6H) shed sets back into the yard after working a Class 'E' turn. The shed is quite full with locomotives occupying most roads. On the Down passenger loop line, rebuilt Royal Scot Class 4-6-0 No.**46154** *The Hussar* stands at the head of a train for Holyhead.
                                                                                          C.J. Clay.

No.51. Bangor (Motive Power Yard). 1964. The Motive Power Yard was cramped and space was at a premium. Consequently wagons had to be moved around to wherever space could be found, once they had been discharged. Here Ivatt 2-6-2T No.**41233** draws a wagon clear of No.1 shed road into the headshunt, and presumably will set back elsewhere in the yard. Normally such wagon movements with the doors left open would be discouraged, but in the absence of supervision, no doubt someone overlooked the error! *Norman Kneale.*

No.52. Bangor M.P.D. c.1964. Class 5 4-6-0 No.**45298**, sporting a hand painted shed code on the smokebox door, and complete with self-weighing tender stands on the loco coal siding road ahead of some wagons, possibly parked at some convenient spot. On Summer Saturdays, parking space was at a premium and congestion at the shed disk was the norm, all lines converging opposite No.2. signal box. The loco was transferred to Bangor in week commencing 20th June 1964, having spent the previous sixteen years at Shrewsbury, although not necessarily coupled to this tender for the entire period. It remained at Bangor until the shed closed on 14th June 1965, when it moved to Holyhead for five months before taking up residence at Mold Junction. The state of the track in the yard left much to be desired, as can be seen, and derailments due to the poor condition were not unknown, with two in one day (always a Summer Saturday) on two, possibly three occasions. Over the wall can be seen two 2-6-4T locomotives in steam, ready to take up their working. *Norman Kneale.*

No.53. Bangor (Motive Power Yard). November 1952. Several Fowler 0-6-0 tender engines had been based at Bangor since 1929 and in the twenty years between 1938 and 1958 the same two engines, Nos. 44305 and 44445 resided at the shed although there was only one specified engine turn for most of this time. In the summer of 1949, this was somewhat surprisingly listed amongst the Passenger Engine Workings, shown as Turn 4, although the passenger content was limited to the 12.45pm Saturdays Only job from Holyhead to Bangor. The rest of the week it was employed on the Nantlle goods. The second engine covering the daily Ballast and Engineering duties which varied from day to day, and when not booked out on this, could be found on Shed duties. No.44445 shunts the Motive Power yard on Saturday morning in 1952, which, according to the majority of the traincrews, was all it was fit for! *W.G. Rear.*

No.54. Bangor (Motive Power Yard). November 1952. An Austerity 2-8-0 No.90317 of Mold Junction shed (6B) stands on No.1. shed road placing wagons of fire bricks in a convenient place for unloading. It had worked west with the early morning freight to Menai Bridge, where it had detached and run light engine back to the shed. Later in the day it would be turned and work east later that evening. For most of the day it was not required. The use of large locomotives for menial tasks like a quick shunt was not unusual; it was in steam and immediately available, and that was sufficient. Bob 'Joy' Williams stands with Arthur and Pat Holbrook who visited the shed with the author to see old friends and colleagues on a rare Saturday 'day off'. *W.G. Rear.*

No.55. Bangor (Motive Power Depot). 1964. An assortment of tank engines rest on Bangor shed during the summer of 1964 whilst the photographer comes under scrutiny from the staff. No.84001 was a Llandudno Junction based engine, arriving in 1962 from Warrington and was withdrawn for scrapping from the Junction in week commencing 31st October 1964 after a very brief working life, These vacuum controlled 2-6-2T engines were used for push-pull trains over the Amlwch branch in its final year of operation, the line having reverted to steam for passenger services after eight years of DMU dominance. The adjoining Fairburn 2-6-4T No.42075 spent several periods at Bangor, finally arriving on 30th June 1964 from Birkenhead, and after a four month stay, moved on loan to Stoke and Aston before withdrawal in May 1965. Details of the Stanier and Fairburn tank engines beyond are unknown. *Norman Kneale.*

No.56. Bangor (Motive Power Yard). 1963. The romance of the steam locomotive is shrouded by myths that were presented in the periodicals of the day, and the harsh reality of shed life rarely mentioned. Certainly the conditions in which the footplate and mechanical staff worked in the declining days of steam were usually primitive, and the experience of staff tested to the limits to keep engines operational. Here Driver Moi Edwards of Caernarfon and a fitter's mate watch as the fitter strips down the rear cylinder drain cock to clear a blockage on Class Five 4-6-0 No.**45328**, which would have come to light during the driver's routine inspection of his engine before going off shed. Note the flare lamp, the wrench and assorted hand tools on the floor, probably the basic emergency repairs toolkit, for such incidents as this. Grime and dirt were accepted as part and parcel of normal operating conditions, as was the necessity to work in the open, whether the weather was fine or otherwise, usually otherwise, and defects could occur at any time of the day or night. Only the driver's vigilance could detect such defects whilst still on shed, otherwise the fault would have to been tolerated/ endured until the completion of the locomotives turn of duty.

Norman Kneale.

No.57. Bangor (Motive Power Depot). 1964. Stanier 2-6-4T No.**42446** stands on No.1 shed road out of steam, and near the end of its life, being finally withdrawn from Bangor in week commencing 25th April 1964 for scrapping. The shed plate had been removed, and apart from the graffiti on the tank side, little paintwork shows through the grime and dirt accumulated over long periods of time, although the locomotive is probably in good mechanical order. Notice the corrosion on the smoke vent chutes, the effect of smoke discharge from the chimneys of locomotives standing underneath. The vents extended the length of the shed and were designed so that the chimney was enclosed by the vent whilst inside the shed. At Bangor, the vents were replaced only six years previously when the cladding on the shed front was renewed at the same time. *Norman Kneale.*

No.58. Bangor (Motive Power Depot). 1964. B.R. Standard Class 3MTT No.**82033** stands at the blocks on No.1 shed road out of steam, awaiting boiler washout and the "X" examination. Three of these engines were transferred to Bangor from Machynlleth in 1960 with a fourth engine following in 1963, as replacements for the Stanier 2-6-2T engines, which worked an assortmentof passenger and shunting turns. It is still sporting Western Region lamp brackets. This locomotive's stay at Bangor was brief, from mid June 1964 until the first week in June 1965 when it was transferred to Nine Elms. Notice the smoke dispersal arrangements in the shed roof previously mentioned. The Engine and Enginemen's Arrangements board is on the wall, illuminated by a cowled lamp, together with several small notice cases.

Norman Kneale.

No.59. Bangor (Motive Power Yard). January 1963. Stranger in the camp! ex LNWR 0-8-0 Class G2a No.**48895** of Bushbury Shed shunts a 3F 0-6-0T in Bangor shed yard prior to taking up its afternoon freight working from Menai Bridge yard to Mold Junction. Birmingham Area engines were uncommon this far west, and it is assumed that it was 'borrowed' off its rostered diagram whilst at Crewe South or Mold Junction. Certainly the crew would not have been too pleased to have this venerable steed in place of the usual Class 5. Notice the open headlamp hiding behind the rail near the tender footsteps. Had the fireman gone to fill the burner sump?

Norman Kneale.

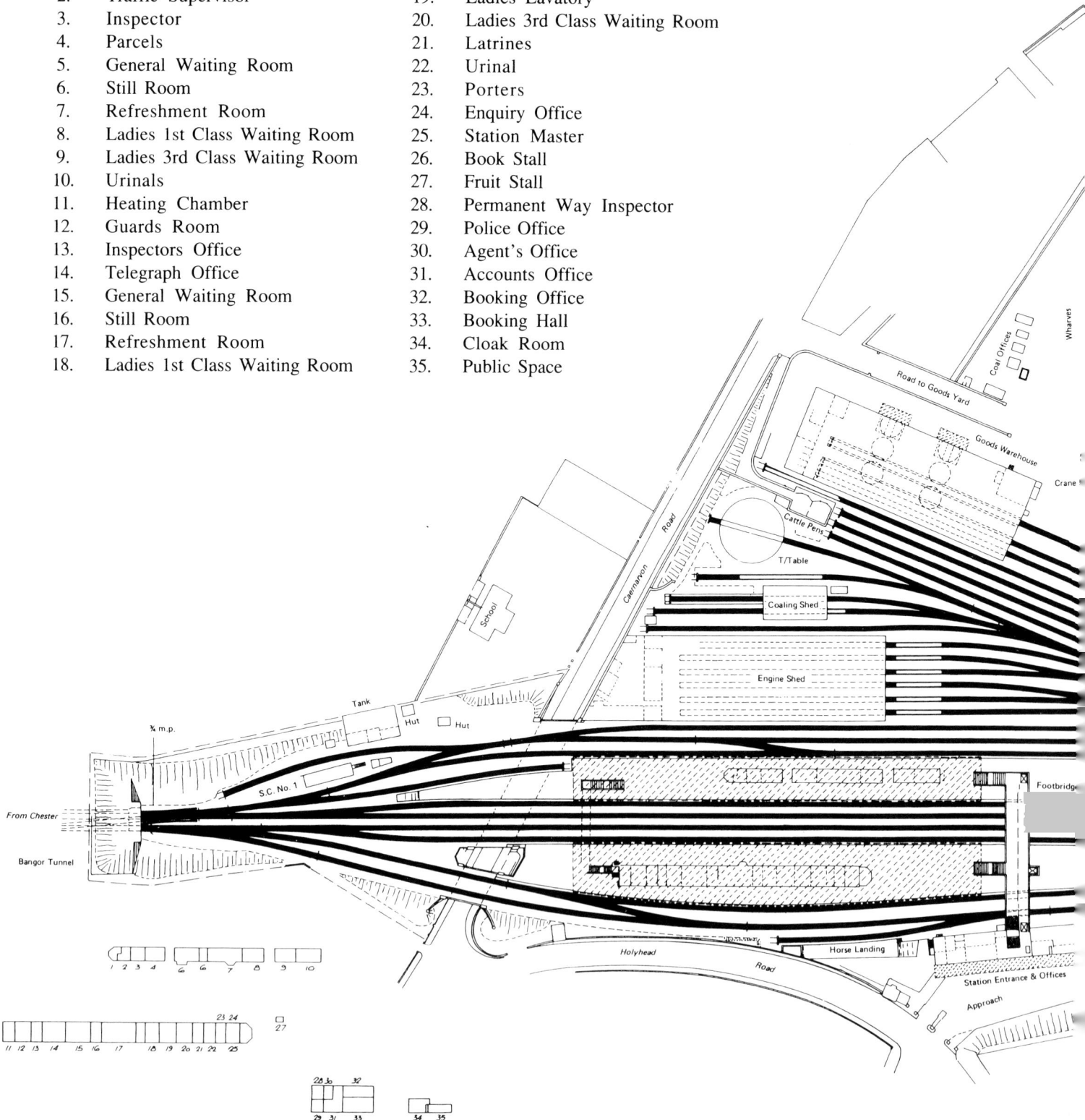

Key to Buildings

1. Inspector
2. Traffic Supervisor
3. Inspector
4. Parcels
5. General Waiting Room
6. Still Room
7. Refreshment Room
8. Ladies 1st Class Waiting Room
9. Ladies 3rd Class Waiting Room
10. Urinals
11. Heating Chamber
12. Guards Room
13. Inspectors Office
14. Telegraph Office
15. General Waiting Room
16. Still Room
17. Refreshment Room
18. Ladies 1st Class Waiting Room
19. Ladies Lavatory
20. Ladies 3rd Class Waiting Room
21. Latrines
22. Urinal
23. Porters
24. Enquiry Office
25. Station Master
26. Book Stall
27. Fruit Stall
28. Permanent Way Inspector
29. Police Office
30. Agent's Office
31. Accounts Office
32. Booking Office
33. Booking Hall
34. Cloak Room
35. Public Space

BANGOR. LMS Station Layout c.1926

Scale: 1 inch = 132 ft.

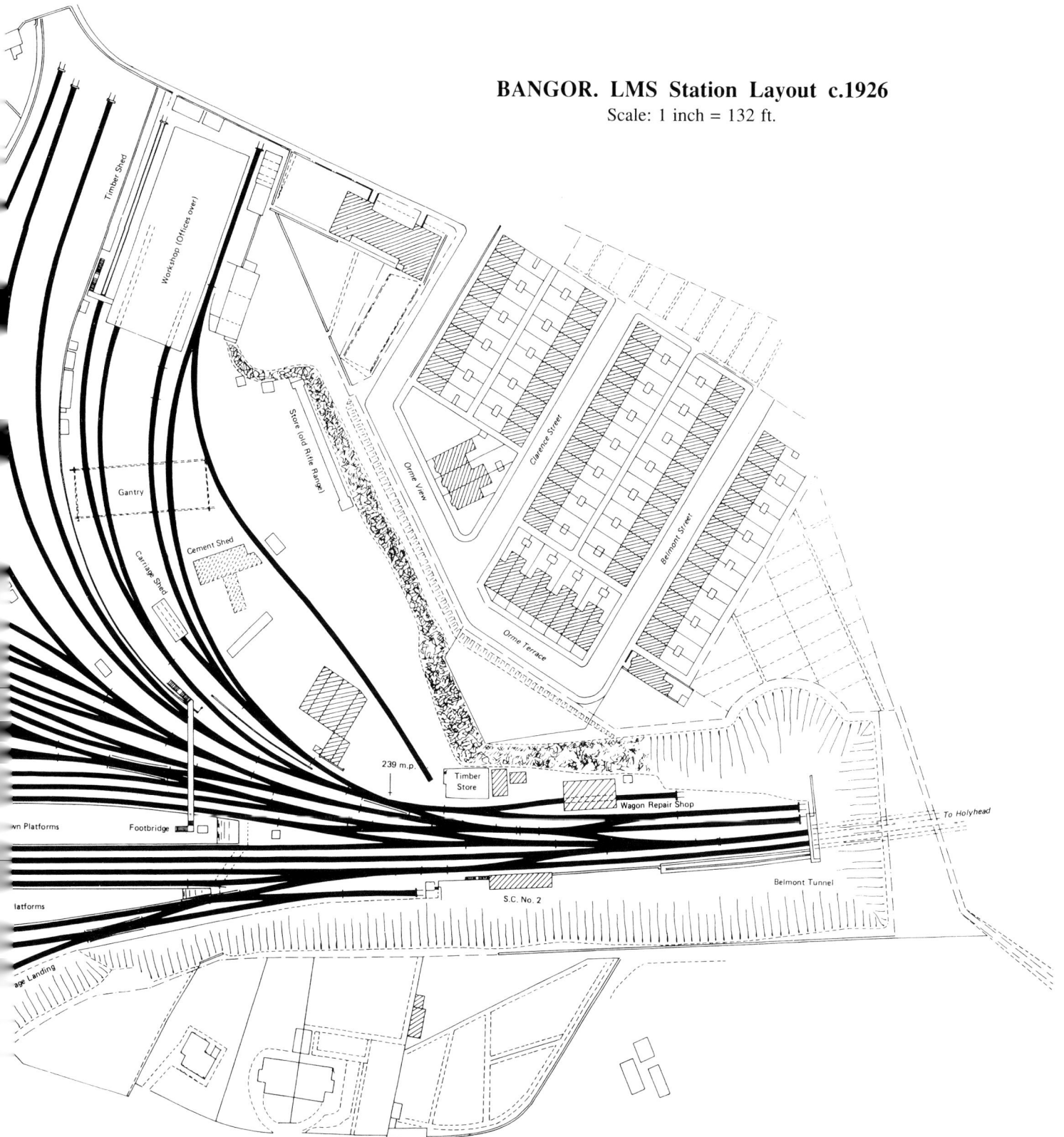

Timber Shed

Workshop (Offices over)

Store (old Rifle Range)

Gantry

Carriage Shed

Cement Shed

Orme View

Clarence Street

Belmont Street

Orme Terrace

239 m.p.

Timber Store

Wagon Repair Shop

To Holyhead

Belmont Tunnel

wn Platforms

Footbridge

latforms

S.C. No. 2

age Landing

No.60. Bangor. Up platform. 1938.
George V Class 4-4-0 No.**5354** *New Zealand* stands at the Up platform with a local for Rhyl. The original Chester & Holyhead Railway stone carved monogram can be seen mounted on the wall under the shade of the canopy.   *G.H. Platt.*

No.61. Bangor. 1st May 1980. A close-up view of the stone carving depicted in the previous view.
Philip J. Kelly.

No.62. Bangor. Up Platform. 13th June 1967. The length of the Up platform is brought out in this view taken from the Down side. The original Thompson building is masked by the canopy but some idea of the style can be gleaned from this view.
A.R. Addey.

No.63. Bangor. Station exterior.
The rebuilding and extending of the station in 1924 provided for a rearrangement of the station forecourt, with the new booking hall predominant. Entrance was through ornamental wrought iron gates, but rarely if ever were they closed to road traffic. The Booking Hall is in the left wing of the building and the parcels and luggage office on the right. A parcels van stands in the Carriage Landing. *British Railways.*

No.64. Bangor. Station exterior.
Passenger entrance to the platforms from the Booking Hall was up this wide flight of stairs which led to the footbridge. At the top of the stairs was a ticket barrier, permanently manned. A luggage lift conveyed barrows and trolleys from ground floor level to the footbridge, and lift shafts were located on the two island platforms. As was the custom, enamel Astons advertisement signs were strategically placed on the stair risers, a feature and firm that were common to most stations throughout North Wales. Notice the style of brickwork, the window design and the embellishments on the canopy boards and on either side of the clock. *British Railways.*

No.65. Bangor. Down Platform.
There were Refreshment Rooms on both platforms although they were hardly commodious. Here on the Down platform the facilities were at the Llandudno Junction end of the platform in the centre of the block. The end building was the General Waiting Room. The walls of the Motive Power Depot can just be seen across the tracks. The Refreshment Room sign is located suspended from the roof, and not very prominently displayed. More conspicuous are the enamel advertising signs, with nationally distributed ones such as Stephens Inks and Virol prominently displayed, but at local level, the Astons signs were to be found wherever there was a space.   *British Railways.*

No.66. Bangor. Down Platform.
Further along the platform at the Holyhead end was the Ladies First Class Waiting Room, and beyond that the Gents! The columns supporting the roof were used to carry away the rain water which drained away below platform level. Notice the abundance of signs, some ageless, others now very much dated.   *British Railways.*

No.67. Bangor. Down Platform.
The canopy over the Down platform extended back towards the Bangor tunnel end, mainly to give some protection over the stairs that led from the passenger subway, some shelter to passengers travelling to Bethesda, whose motor train ran into a bay, beyond the subway stairs. Here the stair guard rails are visible, and this view shows the extent of the platform. A set of suburban coaches stand in the carriage siding, with the Motive Power Depot wall beyond. collection
G.K. Fox.

No.68. Bangor. Down Platform. 13th June 1967. The 1924 footbridge spanning the tracks was extra wide, and the stairs took up most of the platform width. Adjoining the footbridge was the lift shaft, with the towers just visible behind the covering. In the Down Passenger Loop platform a Class 47 stands at the head of a parcels train from Chester. A DMU in plain blue livery stands in the Down Carriage Siding. *A.R. Addey.*

No.69. Bangor. Up Platform. 13th June 1967. When the Up platform was rebuilt in 1924, it was necessary to give sufficient width to accommodate the former main station building and allow adequate platform space for the passengers. This view, taken under the canopy and looking towards Holyhead shows the wide double staircase leading to the passenger footbridge. On the right of the picture, beyond the coach can be seen the back of the parcels building in the Booking Hall complex. Notice also the station furniture, including the letter box. In common with the Down platform, the roof supports served as a drain for the rain water from the glazed roof. *A.R. Addey.*

No.70. Bangor. Up Platform. 13th June 1967. The original Up platform was unchanged during the rebuilding of the station in 1924, and the wide expanse contrasts with the narrow width on the Down side. The canopy extended over the track and gave good protection to passengers. By this time there were comparatively few signs suspended from the roof. However a telephone facility was provided and the old style phone box is a reminder of the past. *A.R. Addey.*

No.71. Bangor (Up Goods Loop Line). June 1952. Liverpool Edge Hill (8A) locomotives were not uncommon at Bangor but these were normally Class Five 4-6-0's. However on this occasion No.**45647** *Sturdee* had worked the 9.20am from Crewe to Holyhead and then worked back on a local as far as Bangor, where it was scheduled to work back the 3.50pm to Crewe. The loco was not long off the works and the paintwork was very clean. Every joint was tight and it rode like a sewing machine on the Down journey.   *W.G. Rear.*

No.72. Bangor. 1954. The North Wales Coast line is synonymous with 'The Irish Mail' and was for many years the exclusive preserve of Royal Scot class locomotives. These trains ran throughout the year, departing Holyhead about 1.10am for Euston with the equivalent Down working departing Euston about 8.45pm. They connected with the boat, due Holyhead about Midnight, and which returned to Dun Laoghaire at 3.25am. During summer months a second daily sea crossing was made, arriving Holyhead about 12.35pm, returning to Eire at 2.30pm. The Day 'Irish Mail' trains ran in each direction, timed to connect with this journey. The 'Up' train departed Holyhead about 1.25pm and crossed the Down train east of Bangor and which arrived at Holyhead at 1.53pm. The loading of these trains was very heavy, the Marshalling Diagram specifying 14 vehicles, 444 tons, although at times extended to 17 vehicles 530 tons. Here No.**46157** *The Royal Artilleryman* of Holyhead Shed (6J) storms through the Up Fast line at Bangor with 14 coaches and a van, in the charge of Holyhead men. An evocative scene, sadly alas no more, replaced by the soul-less HST units that appeared in September 1991.
                                                                    E. Treacy. J.M. Dunn collection.

Coach Working

Information on local coach working based at Bangor in the earliest days is non existent, and through coach working is very sketchy. The earliest 'Diagram of Carriage Working' to hand, covering all the coaching sets based at Bangor, dates from 21st September 1925, although some additional information on Inter District sets working into the area is given in the LNWR 'North Eastern District Carriage Diagram' dated 6th February 1922. The reprint of the LNWR Marshalling Diagram for through carriages dated July, August & September 1910 gives some indication of the corridor stock that worked through the station. The Marshalling and Carriage Working Diagrams were published coincidentally with the issue of Working Time Tables and four publications were produced each occasion, covering the LMS Western, Midland, Central and Northern Divisions. The LNWR style of presentation was modified by 1925, possibly sooner. It should also be noted that the LNWR referred to their Guards compartment vehicles as Break vehicles, but this was modified to the more conventional Brake after the grouping. Marshalling Circulars are still published to this day, albeit in a greatly modified form to reflect the modern traffic requirements. The Local Diagrams of Carriage Workings were letter-press printed in book form until September 1933 when the practice was discontinued. After that date the details were issued as Roneo Duplicated sheets. Modifications to the diagram workings were produced in Rolling Stock Diagram booklets issued regularly from Easter until October, with occasional issues outside these periods.

Below are examples taken from various issues of official publications which relate directly to coach working at Bangor.

Main Line Corridor Coach Workings.

A typical LNWR Main Line working, extracted from the Marshalling Circular for July, August & September 1910 is as follows:

11.30am from Bangor 11.50am from Llandudno (9.30am from Portmadoc) (9.50am from Pwllheli) (Corridor Train) (Commences July 16th)		Balanced at
Break Carriage	} Bangor to	10.45am
Third Class	} London	
1st Class Dining Car (65ft)[A]	} Bangor to	11B15am
2nd & 3rd Dining Car (65ft)	} London	
Break Tri Composite (57ft)	} Pwllheli to	11.15am
	} London	
Tri Composite (57ft)	} Portmadoc to	11.15am
Break Third (57ft)	} London	
Break Third (57ft)	} Llandudno	11.15am
Tri Composite (57ft)	} to	
Tri Composite (57ft)	} London	
Break Third (57ft)	}	

Nuneaton to attach the through carriage, Buxton to London, off the 2.35pm from Burton	11.00am
Rugby to attach Break Tri Composite (42ft) from	-

Warwick to London in rear.

A Returns on the 2.35pm from Bangor from August 6th to September 17th inclusive

B These two cars work light at 5.30pm to Holyhead to be gassed, and return at 9.50am next morning to Bangor.

Two other workings from Bangor are listed in the same programme, namely the 1.45pm Bangor to Birmingham, which combines with the 2.00pm from Llandudno at the Junction. The other working was the 2.35pm from Bangor to Euston, which attached three coaches from Caernarfon and a further four vehicles at Llandudno Junction. In the two latter workings, the stock was dispersed at destination and returned in a variety of workings the following day.

L.M.S. WESTERN DIVISION MARSHALLING CIRCULAR

Commencing May 3rd 1926 and until further notice.

Marshalling		Balance
9.20am., BANGOR TO LIVERPOOL (Lime Street)		
Third (50ft)	{ Bangor to { Liverpool (L.St.)	4.15 pm
M. & L. Set (4 vehicles)	{ Pwllheli to { Liverpool (L.St.)	C. D.
bBreak Van (32ft) (Milk)	{ Amlwch to { Llandudno	
	Attach front Llandudno Junction:-	
aM. & L. Set (4 vehicles)	} Llandudno to } Manchester	C. D. 10.50am
aBrake Van (30ft)	} (Exchange)	
	6 veh. 148 Tons from Bangor 10 veh. 269 Tons from Llandudno Junc. 5 veh. 135 Tons from Chester	

a Received off 9.45am from Llandudno. Transferred Chester to 11.45am to Manchester.
b Received off 7.55am from Amlwch. Transferred Llandudno Junc. to 10.38am to Llandudno.

1.10pm., BANGOR TO MANCHESTER (Exchange		
S Inter-District Set (4 (N.C.) vehicles)	} Bangor to } } Llandudno Junct. }	
M. & L. Set (4 vehicles)	{ Bangor to } { Manchester } { Exchange }	C. D.
	Attach from Llandudno Junction :- }	
aStoke Lavatory Set (5 (N.C.) vehicles	} Llandudno to } Derby	
	8 veh. 220 Tons (S) from Bangor 4 veh. 110 Tons (SO) from Bangor 9 veh. 237 Tons from Llandudno Junc. 4 veh. 110 Tons from Chester	

a Received off 1.35pm from Llandudno. Transferred Chester to 3.22pm to Derby.

3.01pm, BANGOR TO LIVERPOOL (Lime Street)

cH.M.& L. Set (2 vehs)	} Holyhead to	C. D.
cMSO Third (57ft)	} Liverpool (L.St.)	-
dBreak Composite (57ft)	{ Portmadoc to	10.45am
	{ Liverpool (L.St.)	
adBreak Composite (57ft)	{ Portmadoc to	10.50am
	{ Manchester (Ex.)	
adBreak Composite (57ft)	{ Pwllheli to	10.50am
	{ Manchester (Ex.)	
Attach front Llandudno Junction:-		
bM.& L. Set (4 vehicles)	{ Llandudno to	C. D.
	{ Liverpool (L.St.)	

5 Veh. 152 Tons. (MS) from Bangor
6 Veh. 182 Tons. (MSO) from Bangor
9 Veh. 292 Tons. (MS) from Llandudno Jc.
10 Veh. 292 Tons. (MSO) from Llandudno Jc.
7 Veh. 194 Tons. (MS) from Chester
8 Veh. 224 Tons. (MSO) from Chester

a Transferred Chester to 5.13pm Manchester Ex
b Received off 3.20pm from Llandudno
c Received off 1.30pm from Holyhead
d Received off 1.13pm from Afonwen

LMS WESTERN DIVISION MARSHALLING CIRCULAR
May 1st 1939 until further notice.

10.32am (SO), BANGOR TO EUSTON
(Class "A" Stock)

Composite (18/24)	} Euston	5FO20 pm
Third Brake	}	
Attach rear Llandudno Junction:-		
aThird Brake (24)	}	
aThird Vestibule (60ft)	}	
aKitchen Car	}	
aFirst Vestibule (57ft)	} Llandudno-Euston	
aComposite (18/24)	}	
aThird Brake (24)	}	
bThird (42)	} Pwllheli-Euston	
bCompo.Brake (12/21)	}	

a Received off 11.00am from Llandudno
b Received off 9.25am from Afonwen

Tonnage -   61 Bangor
           314 Llandudno Junction

12.10pm. BANGOR TO LIVERPOOL (Lime Street)

Inter-Corridor Set	}	B.
(3 vehicles)	} Liverpool (L.St.)	
H.M.& L. Set (SO)	}	
(2 vehicles)	}	
aH.M.& L. Set (SX)	{ Afonwen to	
(2 vehicles)	{ Liverpool (L.St.)	
AacCompo.Brake(SX)(12/21)	} Pwllheli-Euston	
cComposite (18/24) (MSX)	{Bangor-Euston	5.20pm (FSX)
Attach rear Chester:-		
AbCompo.Brake (SX)(12/21)	} Holyhead-	
	Liverpool (L.St.)	

a Received off 10.48am from Afonwen

---

b Received off 12.40pm from Holyhead
c Transferred Chester to 12.40pm Holyhead to Euston
   B 7.20am, from Manchester (Exchange)

Tonnage-   **175 (SX), 145 (SO) Bangor**
             175 (SX), 145 (SO) Chester

BRITISH RAILWAYS LONDON MIDLAND REGION (Western Division)
PASSENGER TRAIN MARSHALLING

14th June to 19th September inclusive 1954.

Marshalling			Balance
12.45pm (SX) BANGOR TO EUSTON			
(Runs until 9th July inclusive and			
commences 13th September)			
(Class "A" Stock)			
2-TK	(42)	}	
Y TO	(56)	} }	B
Y R F	(24)	}Euston }	
2-CK	(18/24)	} }	C
BTK	(24)	} }	
Attach front Llandudno Junction:			
a BTK	(24)	}	
a 2-CK	(18/24)	} Llandudno-Euston	
a TK	(42)	}	

a   Received off 1.00pm from Llandudno
B.   11.00am (SX) from Holyhead.
       Works 5.15pm (MSX) , 5.20pm (SO)
           Euston to Holyhead
C.   11.00am (SX) from Holyhead.
       Work 10.50am (SX) Euston to Holyhead

BANGOR   -   7/231
LLANDUDNO JUNCTION   -   11/355

4.10pm (SO) BANGOR TO BIRMINGHAM

10 Corridor Vehicles - Birminghan	Divl R. Crewe.
10/310	

4.47pm (SX) BANGOR TO HOLYHEAD
(Runs 12th July to 10th Sept. inclusive)

Z BTK	(24)	}	
Z CK	(24/18)	} Holyhead	B.
Y R F	(24)	}	
Y TO	(56)	}	

B.   11.15am (SX) from Euston.
       Work 11.00am (MSX) }
              10.45am (SO)   } Holyhead to Bangor

       4/143

4.47pm (SO) BANGOR TO HOLYHEAD
(Marshalling until 10th July incl. and on
   18th September)

Z BTK	(24)	}Holyhead }	B.

Z	CK	(24/18) }		}		
B.	11.15am (SO) from Holyhead Work 10.45am (SO) Holyhead to Bangor until 10th July, 11.00am (MO) Holyhead to Bangor. 12th July 2/67					

4.47pm (SO) BANGOR TO HOLYHEAD
(Marshalling 17th July to 11the September)

Z	BTK	(24) }		}		B.
Z	CK	(24/18) }		}		
Y	RF	(24) }	Holyhead	}		
Y	TO	(56) }		}		C.

B.   11.15am (SO) from Euston.
Work 11.00am (MO) Holyhead to Bangor
until 6th September incl. 10.45am (SO)

C.   11.15am (SO) from Euston.
Work 11.00am (MO) Holyhead to Bangor
until 6th September inclusive.

4/143

Local Coach Workings

The London & North Western Railway allocated its local carriage working sets into the various Districts, producing printed books listing the workings which coincided with the working time table issues. Both the LNWR and LMS referred to the local workings as chained up sets which is interpreted as an formation of vehicles which were kept together, permanently coupled, although obviously vehicles were replaced for service or repair from time to time and their place in the set would be taken by a similar vehicle. As the older vehicles were withdrawn from service, the replacement vehicles would be of more up to date design and the District requirements would reflect this change.

Local coach workings up to and at the time of the Grouping tended to be kept to shorter workings. The more modern bogie vehicles were allocated to Inter District workings which comprised 4 vehicles and weighed 110 tons and, as such, followed set circuit diagrams and worked further from the home station. In the **1922 Diagram of Carriage Working** book these were listed as sets 1 to 221, but in fact there were only 192 working sets in this category. Most sets were on limited workings, the circuits of which varied from one to seven days before re-commencing, whilst the older stock, including four and six wheel vehicles worked mainly around to their home district on one, two or three day workings.

INTER DISTRICT SET WORKINGS. (IDZ)
6th February 1922 until further notice.
London & North Western Railway North Eastern District Inter District Sets working into North Wales numbered 153 to 173. These comprised Chester & Holyhead Sets (153-157); Manchester and Llandudno Corridor Sets (Nos.158/9 - 5 vehicles)(Nos.160/1/2 - 4 vehicles); Llandudno, Manchester and Crewe Sets (163/163a/164/5 - 3 vehicles); Manchester and Carnarvon Set (166 - 5 vehicles); Manchester and Holyhead Set 167/8/9/70). Sets 170-180 were single or two coach sets which worked

as through coaches to destination attached to other workings. Of direct interest to this work was Set Nos. 154 and 157 which terminated at Bangor and were allocated to Manchester Exchange. Set 154 started its day at Chester and worked to Exchange at 9.10am. The stock was stored at Ordsall Lane during the day, and then worked the 7.10pm to Chester, due 9.05pm, and worked forward on the 9.40pm to Bangor, due 11.25pm. It departed for Chester the next day at 1.15pm, working No.164, and after four hours wait in Exchange, worked back to Holyhead arriving at 1.10am. departing back to Exchange on Circuit 159 at 2.20am. Circuit Set 166 worked from Exchange to Caernarvon, arriving at 11.44am and departed for Chester at 3.35pm. After a short wait it formed the 7.43pm to Exchange. This was repeated daily. Circuit set 168 departed Exchange at 4.45pm arriving in Bangor at 8.00pm, and returned to Exchange the following day at 9.20am. At the Grouping, the local carriage workings were regrouped into the various Divisions as mentioned previously. The design and layout of the book was different to the LNWR versions, and contained a lot more detail. Traffic working out of and into Bangor totalled 28 sets which came under various categories according to the working. Inter District sets comprised 4 vehicles - 110 tons. (3 sets), Manchester & Llandudno sets, 4 vehicles - 113 tons; Bangor District (8 sets) 5 vehicles - 65 tons; Chester & Holyhead (7 sets) 5 vehicles - 96 tons; Holyhead, Manchester & Liverpool (7 sets) 2 vehicles - 52 tons; Llandudno Junction & Afonwen, 1 set 2 vehicles - 26 tons. Sets were available for strengthening purposes (Nos.828 to 843) in various configurations and sets from other districts appeared at Bangor as part of their normal schedule. In addition to the above vehicles, Motor Train stock was also listed. Set 845 comprised a Driving third and third (57 tons) and worked the Bethesda branch service, strengthened at peak times by the addition of four thirds vehicles (52 tons). Set 846 worked the Caernarvon & Llanberis branch, and made an appearance at Bangor daily, as did set 850 - working the Llandudno & Llanfairfechan shuttle, whilst set 854 which worked the Red Wharf Bay service which started and finished at Bangor. The earliest list of Bangor District set working available is from the LMS Western Section issue for 21st September 1925. The workings are as follows:

BANGOR DISTRICT SETS
(5 vehicles 65 tons) Circuits 779 to 786.

No.779 - Worked by 786 (M) and No.786 (MO)

	arr	dep	
Bangor	-	6.45am	
Afonwen	8.05am	8.32	
Pwllheli.........	8.42	9.30	A.
Afonwen	9.40	9.50	
Bangor	11.15	12.02pm	
Afonwen	1.35	4.00	B.
Bangor	5.27	-	

A -   Also break composite Euston.
B -   R. Manchester (Ex) in front.
Works No.784 (M) and 784 (MO).

No.780 - Worked by No.785 and No.781

	arr	dep	
Amlwch.........	-	7.55am	A.
Bangor	9.02am	11.08	
Amlwch.........	12.13pm	1.10pm	
Gaerwen	1.50	3.35	B.
Amlwch.........	4.42	-	

A -   Two N extras (FO).
B -   Leaves at 3.50pm (ThO).
Works No.781 (M) and No.781 (MO)

No.781 - Worked by No.780 (M) and No.784 (MO)

	arr	dep	
Amlwch.........	-	3.50pm	
Gaerwen	4.41pm	5.30	SO
Amlwch.........	6.25	7.10	SO
Gaerwen	7.57	8.01	SO
Bangor	8.18	9.25	SO
Gaerwen	9.41	9.43	SO
Amlwch.........	10.30	-	

Works No.786 (M) and No.780 (MO)

No.782 - Worked by No.784 (M) and No.784 (MO)

	arr	dep	
Bangor	-	4.46am	
Pwllheli.........	6.35am	6.45	
Bangor	8.25	11.08	SO
Gaerwen	11.24	1.13pm	SO
Amlwch.........	2.02pm	2.13	SO
Gaerwen	2.55	3.00	SO
Bangor	3.17	3.30	SO
Gaerwen	3.47	-	
Bangor	-	3.20	S
Afonwen	5.13	5.32	S
Bangor	6.59	8.55	S
Carnarvon	9.20	-	

Works No.785 (M) and No.786 (MO)

No.783 - Worked by No.783 (M) and No.785 (MO)

	arr	dep	
Bangor	-	9.55am	
Llandudno Jn.	10.31am	11.48	S
Bangor	12.30pm	-	
Llandudno Jn.	-	12.28pm	SO
Bangor	1.05	3.20	SO
Afonwen	5.13	5.32	SO
Bangor	6.59	9.20	SO
Carnarvon	9.45	9.55	SO
Nantlle	10.28	10.35	SO
Carnarvon	11.02	-	

Works No.783 (M) and No.785 (MO)

No.784 - Worked by No.779 (M) and No.779 (MO)

	arr	dep	
Bangor	-	8.10am	
Llandudno Jn.	8.47am	11.48	S
Bangor	12.30pm	-	
Llandudno Jn.	-	12.28pm	SO
Bangor	1.05	1.10	
Carnarvon	1.37	4.30	
Bangor	4.56	5.47	
Carnarvon	6.12	6.35	
Bangor	6.59	-	

Works No.782 (M) and No. 782 (MO)

No.785 - Worked by No.782 (M) and No.783 (MO)

	arr	dep		
Carnarvon	-	11.48am		
Bangor	12.13pm	12.50pm	ThO	
Llangefni	1.24	3.35	ThO	
Bangor	4.05	5.00	S.	
Gaerwen	5.17	5.30	S.	A.
Amlwch.........	6.25	7.10	S.	
Gaerwen	7.57	9.15	S.	B.
Amlwch.........	9.58	-		
Bangor	-	12.55	SO	
Rhyl	1.58	6.00	SO	
Llandudno Jn.	6.33	6.38	SO	
Bangor	7.22	-		

A - 2 N extra (ThO)
B - 2 N extra (WO)
Works No.780 (M) and No.783 (MO)

No.786 - Worked by No.781 (M) and No.782 (MO)

	arr	dep		
Gaerwen	-	5.20am		
Amlwch.........	6.35am	7.00		
Gaerwen	7.59	9.30		A
Amlwch.........	10.15	11.10		B
Gaerwen	12.14pm	12.45pm		
Bangor	1.03	1.55	SO	
Bethesda	2.13	2.22	SO	
Bangor	2.40	4.53		C
Afonwen	6.07	7.02		
Bangor	8.35	-		

A - N and O extra (ThO)
B - 2 N extra (ThO)
C - Also break composite, Euston to Pwllheli
Works No.779 (M) and No.779 (MO).

Codes used in the diagrams:
     S = Saturdays Excepted. SO = Saturdays Only
     R = Brake Van. N = Third Class. O = Third Brake.
It will be noted that much of the stock used were non bogie
vehicles

BRITISH RAILWAYS

SPECIAL CHEAP DAY TICKETS
EACH WEEKDAY

UNTIL FURTHER NOTICE

TO

CAERNARVON

AND

BANGOR

BY ANY TRAIN

FROM	RETURN FARE—SECOND CLASS	
	To CAERNARVON	To BANGOR
	s. d.	s. d.
ABERERCH	4/3	6/-
AFON WEN	3/9	5/6
CRICCIETH	4/3	6/-
PENRHYNDEUDRAETH	5/6	7/3
PENYCHAIN	4/-	5/9
PORTMADOC	4/9	6/6
PWLLHELI	4/9	6/3

(FIRST CLASS TICKETS WILL BE ISSUED AT 50% OVER ABOVE FARE)

Children under Three years of age. Free: Three and under Fourteen years of age, Half-fare.

PASSENGERS MAY RETURN BY ANY TRAIN SAME DAY
AFFORDING A SERVICE THROUGH TO DESTINATION.

NOTICE AS TO CONDITIONS.—These tickets are issued subject to the British Transport Commission's published Regulations and Conditions applicable to British Railways exhibited at their Stations or obtainable free of charge at Station Booking Offices.

Tickets can be obtained in advance at Booking Stations

CIRCULAR TOUR TICKETS FOR BUSINESS OR PLEASURE JOURNEYS AT REDUCED FARES.

Further information will be supplied on application to the Stations or to Mr. O VELTOM, District Traffic Superintendent, Oswestry (Telephone Oswestry 189, Extension 21:), or Mr. E FLAXMAN, Commercial Officer, Paddington Station, W.2.

Paddington Station, W.2.
February, 1958.

No. 8.

Printed in Great Britain by G. R. Griffith Ltd., Chester.

PRE-CHRISTMAS EXCURSION

Saturday 17th December 1960

LEAGUE DIVISION 1
Everton
v.
Tottenham Hotspur
AT GOODISON PARK

SPECIAL EXCURSIONS
TO

LIVERPOOL

Outward Dep'ture	FROM	Return Arrival	RETURN FARE SECOND CLASS
a.m		p.m	s. d.
8A46	AMLWCH	11A27	18/6
8A54	RHOSGOCH	11A20	17/9
9A00	LLANERCHYMEDD	11A14	17/-
9A07	LLANGWLLOG	11A06	16/-
9A13	LLANGEFNI	11A00	15/9
9A23	GAERWEN	10A51	15/-
9A28	LLANFAIR P.G.	10A45	14/3
9 45	BANGOR	10 34	14/-
9C41	LLANFAIRFECHAN	10 23	12/9
9C48	PENMAENMAWR	10 17	12/-
9C56	CONWAY	10 08	11/3
9B48	LLANDUDNO	10B18	11/9
9B54	DEGANWY	10B12	11/3
8B40	BLAENAU FFESTINIOG	11B25	16/-
8B58	DOLWYDDELEN	11B09	15/3
9B14	BETWS-Y-COED	10B39	13/9
9B20	LLANRWST	10B31	13/-
9B31	TALYCAFN	10B19	11/9
10 12	LLANDUDNO JUNCTION	10 05	11/3
10 22	COLWYN BAY	9 56	10/6
10 34	ABERGELE	9 45	9/3
10 44	RHYL	9 37	8/6
10 53	PRESTATYN	9 26	8/-
p.m		r	
12 15	LIVERPOOL LIME STREET	8 00	

NOTES :   A — Passengers change at BANGOR on the outward and return journey.

B — Passengers change at LLANDUDNO JUNCTION on the outward and return journey.

C — Passengers change at LLANDUDNO JUNCTION on the outward journey only.

Children under three years of age, free ; three years and under fourteen, half-fares.

TICKETS CAN BE OBTAINED IN ADVANCE AT STATIONS AND OFFICIAL RAILWAY AGENTS

Further information will be supplied on application to the Stations, Official Railway Agents, or to
K. F. Mason District Traffic Superintendent, Chester. Tel. Chester 24680 (Ext. 28)

LONDON MIDLAND

Oct. 1960 K332   The Deeside Printing Co. Sandycroft Nr. Chester   6 R 3500 0

No.73. Bangor. (Down Passenger Loop platform). June 1952. Rhyl shed (7D) 4-4-0 No.**40580** stands at the platform having arrived with the 9.00am all stations from Chester to Bangor one bright Saturday morning. These locomotives were ideally suited to the three coach workings that constituted the local element of traffic along the coast. This locomotive came from Wigan to Rhyl in May 1951, initially on loan, but made permanent from 23rd June of the same year, although it spent most of its days at Denbigh shed, where it was out-stationed. It remained there for four years before transferring to Chester. The loco worked a local through Mold to Chester, where it turned and coupled to the stock off the 7.45am from Liverpool Lime Street, which it worked as far as Bangor where it detached and went on shed to turn. The stock formed the 11.35am to Pwllheli. The loco then worked the 3.10pm local to Llandudno Junction, then worked forward to Rhyl. After turning there once more, it finally worked the 10.35pm train to Denbigh, where it had started its day's work.
W.G. Rear.

There were significant changes to local coach working by 1933, which is the next example available, although it is likely that these changes were introduced gradually over the eight year period. The coaching stock for local workings consisted mainly of pre-grouping design vehicles, and in most cases reflected the pre-grouping parent company, although some of the smaller companies stock disappeared early on, replaced from the reserves of the larger ones. Bangor working stock was predominantly of LNWR design.

The number of Districts had also been reduced by 1933. Inter District Sets now comprised 3 vehicles, weight 84 tons, allocated Circuit Numbers 1 to 243, and a new class of chained up set had been introduced, known as the Lavatory Sets and which comprised 4 vehicles and weighed 108 tons. These were allocated circuit numbers 287 to 358. The Bangor District sets had been dispersed. Circuits 798 to 801 covered the Amlwch branch, and Circuits 808 to 817 were allocated to the Holyhead, Manchester & Liverpool workings, Sets 819 to 832 were the Llandudno District, circuits 833 to 836a and 852 were used between Llandudno Junction and Blaenau Ffestiniog. The working of Motor Train sets had been increased, with 865/66 worked between Bangor, Bethesda, Caernarvon, Colwyn Bay, Llandudno, Llandudno Junction and Rhyl, and set 867 covering the Amlwch branch. Some of the Bangor workings are located within the Inter District sets. Typical examples of an Inter District circuit set is as follows:

No.165a - Worked by No.172c (M) and No.172b (MO).

	arr	dep		
Caernarvon	-	9.28am D.		
Llanberis	9.49am	9.56	D.	
Caernarvon	10.14	12.40pm	D.	
Llanberis	1.01pm	1.15	D.	
Caernarvon	1.33	1.40	S.	
Llandudno Jn.	2.42	2.50	S.	
Llandudno	3.03	3.45	S.	
Llandudno Jn.	3.55	-		
Caernarvon	-	2.40pm	SO.	
Llanberis	3.01pm	3.15	SO.	
Caernarvon	3.33	4.40	SO.	A.
Llanberis	5.00	5.30	SO.	A.
Llandudno Jn.	6.28	6.45	SO.	A.
Llandudno	6.55	7.30	SO.	
Llandudno Jn.	7.40	8.45	SO.	
Llandudno	8.55	-		
Llandudno	-	11.00	Sun.	
Rhyl	12.04pm	7.00pm	Sun.	
Llandudno	7.40	9.05	Sun.	
Colwyn Bay	9.25	10.15	Sun.	
Llandudno	10.35	10.50	Sun.	
Llandudno Jn.	11.00	-		

A -   Observation Car.
Works No.172d (M) and No.172d (MO)

No.168 - Worked by No.174 (M) and No.172d (MO).

	arr	dep	
Llandudno Jn.	-	4.35am	S.
Llandudno	4.44am	9.10	S.
Llandudno Jn.	9.20	9.25	S.
Llanberis	10.43	10.48	S.
Bangor	11.42	12.15pm	S.
Llandudno Jn.	12.46pm	12.55	S.
Llandudno	1.05	1.50	S.
Llandudno Jn.	2.00	2.50	S.
Caernarvon	3.49	5.55	S.
Llanberis	6.16	7.00	S.
Llandudno Jn.	8.14	8.25	S.
Llandudno	8.35	8.55	S.
Llandudno Jn.	9.05	9.15	S.
Caernarvon	10.09	-	
Llandudno Jn.	-	12.25pm	SO.
Colwyn Bay	12.35pm	12.45	SO.
Manchester Ex	2.40	-	SO.
Ordsall Lane	-	6.11	SO.
Manchester Ex	6.16	6.40	SO.
Chester........	7.45	8.02	SO.
Llandudno	9.20	10.30	SO.
Llandudno Jn.	10.39	10.47	SO.
Bangor	11.18	-	
Bangor	-	5.00pm	Sun.
Holyhead	5.53pm	-	Sun.

Works No.174a (M) and No.172e (MO).

No.172a - Worked by No.172e (M) and No.172c (MO).

	arr	dep	
Rhyl	-	6.20am	WO.
Chester........	7.24am	9.12	WO.
Rhyl	9.51	10.15	S.
Llandudno	10.46	11.30	S.
Rhyl	12.10pm	2.20pm	S.
Llandudno	2.51	3.15	S.
Rhyl	4.00	4.40	S.
Holyhead	6.55	7.25	S.
Rhyl	9.17	10.40	WO.
Chester........	11.40	5.52am	ThO.
Rhyl	6.58am	-	
Rhyl	-	11.40am	SO.
Crewe	1.30pm	3.10pm	SO.
Rhyl	5.01	-	

Works No.172 (M) and No.170 (MO)

No.172b - Worked by No.172b (M) and No.174a (MO).

	arr	dep	
Llandudno	-	10.25am	S.
Rhyl	10.54am	1.30pm	S.
Llandudno	2.15pm	2.30	S.
Rhyl	3.01	7.35	S.
Llandudno	8.09	8.30	S.
Llandudno Jn.	8.39	9.55	S.
Llandudno	10.05	-	
Llandudno	-	9.10am	SO.
Llandudno Jn.	9.20am	12.30pm	SO.
Bangor	1.01pm	1.08	SO.
Caernarvon	1.30	4.40	SO.

Llanberis	....	5.00	5.30	SO.
Llandudno Jn.	....	6.28	6.45	SO.
Llandudno	....	6.55	7.15	SO.
Llandudno Jn.	....	7.25	7.37	SO.
Llanberis	....	9.01	9.25	SO.
Caernarvon	....	9.43		

Works No.172b (M) and No.165a (MO).

No.172c - Worked by No. 172d (M) and No. 206 (MO).

		arr	dep		
Llandudno	....	-	10.00am	S.	
Llandudno Jn.	....	10.10am	10.17	S.	
Betws y Coed	.....	10.47	1.00pm	S.	
Llandudno Jn.	....	1.34pm	1.45	S.	
Llandudno	....	1.55	2.10	S.	
Betws y Coed	.....	2.52	5.50	S.	
Llandudno	....	6.45	7.15	S.	
Llandudno Jn.	....	7.25	7.37	S.	
Llanberis	....	9.01	9.20	S.	C.
Caernarvon	....	10.30	-		
Llandudno	....	-	2.35pm	SO.	
Llandudno Jn.	....	2.45pm	2.50	SO.	
Bangor	....	3.24	3.30	SO.	
Caernarvon	....	3.49	7.25	SO.	
Llanberis	....	7.46	8.00	SO.	
Rhyl	....	9.33	-		

C - Freight.
Works No.165a (M) and No. 172a(MO).

No.172d - Worked by No.165a (M) and No.165a (MO)

		arr	dep	
Llandudno Jn.	....	-	12.20pm	S.
Bangor	....	12.59pm	1.08	S.
Llanberis	....	2.00	2.15	S.
Caernarvon	....	2.33	5.55	S.
Llanberis	....	6.16	6.30	S.
Llandudno Jn.	....	7.41	7.50	S.
Llandudno	....	8.02	10.15	S.
Llandudno Jn.	....	10.24	10.35	S.
Llandudno	....	10.47	-	
Llandudno Jn.	....	-	9.25am	SO.
Llanberis	....	10.43am	11.05	SO.
Caernarvon	....	11.23	11.45	SO.
Bangor	....	12.10pm	4.20pm	SO.
Llandudno Jn.	....	4.53	5.00	SO.
Llandudno	....	5.10	6.15	SO.
Llandudno Jn.	....	6.25	-	

Works No. 172c (M) and No. 168 (MO).

No.174a - Worked by No.168 (M) and No.215 (MO).

		arr	dep	
Bangor	....	-	4.15am	MO.
Caernarvon	....	4.28am	4.45	MO.
Afonwen	....	5.33	7.08	D.
Bangor	....	8.21	10.40	D.
Afonwen	....	11.57	9.00pm	S.
Bangor	....	10.09pm	10.15	S.

Llandudno Jn.	....	10.43		
Afonwen	....	-	1.15pm	SO.
Bangor	....	2.26pm	2.35	SO.
Llandudno Jn.	....	3.10	3.47	SO.
Bangor	....	4.22	5.05	SO.
Afonwen	....	6.13	8.15	SO.
Llandudno Jn.	....	10.02	10.10	SO.
Llandudno	....	10.20	11.15	SO.
Colwyn Bay	....	11.30	-	
Colwyn Bay	....	-	2.10pm	Sun.
Holyhead	....	3.58pm	4.45	Sun.
Llandudno Jn.	....	6.14	6.20	Sun.
Betws y Coed	.....	6.55	8.25	Sun.
Llandudno Jn.	....	8.59	9.35	Sun.
Betws y Coed	.....	10.10	10.25	Sun.
Llandudno	....	11.15		

Works 168 (M) and No.172b (MO).

The appointment of W.A. Stanier to the LMS saw the introduction of modern flush sided stock, which included a range of non corridor vehicles. Readers should refer to the definitive histories of LMS coaching stock by Messrs Essery & Jenkinson for specific details. In due course Stanier stock filtered into the local coach sets, and was to be seen at Bangor. With the cessation of printing the 'Diagram of Coach Working' books, up-dating the coach working at Bangor has been difficult to establish. All principal stations involved in providing sets of carriages for local workings were required to keep details of stock working, and Station Masters were required to submit details of their regular daily working in Station Working books, which were updated daily. Regrettably no complete picture of the circuit stocks based at Bangor since the war have come to light, but by methodical study of surviving scraps of information, and perusal of R.S.D. notices, a reasonably accurate picture can be built up, which relates to set numbers which apparantly changed little between 1948 and 1964. Details are given on the next page, but it must be emphasised that this information is not guaranteed 100% accurate. The material abstracted dates from the period commencing 31st May 1948.

An eight page LMS publication entitled Information for the Guidance of Staff dealing with Passenger-Carrying Vehicles dated June 1939 confirmed the view that local coach set composition and workings were rigidly adhered to, although alterations were made over the years to suit the changing traffic requirements. This publication specified that the sets were clipped to keep sets intact. The clip was a device fixed on the draw bar hook which made uncoupling of sets difficult. The instruction was also given that sets were not to be unclipped without the authority of Traffic Department at Crewe except in cases of emergency. Relevant extracts from the above mentioned booklet are given below:

The types of sets in most general use on the Western Division are as follows:-

Corridor Sets
No.of Coaches

Main-Line	...	...	...	...	Varies from 2 to 7 or more
Inter-Corridor ...	...	...	...	...	...	3
Holyhead, Manchester & Liverpool	...	...	...	...	2

Non-corridor Sets
No. of Coaches

Inter-District	...	...	...	...	...	...	...	3
Lavatory	...	...	...	...	...	...	...	3
Two-coach	...	...	...	...	...	.	...	2

Extra Trains.
No. of Coaches

Non-Corridor, Non-Lavatory	...	...	..	8 (clipped throughout)
Non-Corridor, Lavatory	...	...	...	...7 (Clipped throughout)
Corridor	...	...	...	.. 7 (Clipped throughout)
Vestibule	...	...	...	.. 6 (Clipped 3 and 3)
Vestibule	...	...	...	10 (Clipped 3-4-3)

Each set or extra train is end-boarded or end lettered with its description and number.

For example　　　　I.C.S. No.62.
　　　　　　　　　Lavatory Set No.64
　　　　　　　　　2-Coach Set No.22
　　　　　　　　　Extra Train No.78.

In May 1948 six Five-Coach corridor sets worked into and out of Bangor. The composition of the set is not known, only the Circuit Numbers and workings, which were as follows:

Set No.	Working Off	Next Working	Day
127	1/50pm ex Llan. Jn.	4/50pm Llan. Jn.	Saturday
151	1/30pm ex Liverpool	7.35am Birmingham	Sunday
144	11/05pm ex Llan. Jn.	7.35am Birmingham	·Sunday
109	3.15am ex Crewe	3/35pm Llan. Jn.	Sunday
119	9.30am ex Liverpool	6/55pm Liverpool	Sunday
126	9/18pm ex Llan. Jn.	9.40am Crewe	Monday

Circuits based on Bangor in May 1948 were as follows:

3-Coach Sets. non-corridor.		3-Coach Lavatory Sets. non-corridor.	
218	2-day working.	1199	2-day working.
230	2-day working.	1207	2-day working.
235	2-day working.	1220	2-day working.
237	2-day working.	1230	2-day working.
1310	2-day working.	1232	2-day working.
1311	daily.	1235	2-day working.
1316	daily.		

Typical working examples are as follows:

Circuit Set No.230

3-coach set. non-corridor.

arr.	Station	dep.	days	Rep.No.
	Chester	5.45am	MWFO.	15
8.41am	Bangor	9.00	MWFO.	
10.17	Afonwen	10.55	MWFO.	
12/12pm	Bangor	5/25pm	MWFO.	
6/39	Amlwch	7/15	MWFO.	332

9/03	Llandudno Jn.	11/05	MWFO.		
11/38	Bangor.				
	Bangor	6.40am	TThO.		ECS
7.06am	Caernarvon	7.15	TThO.	52	
8.33	Llandudno	10.00	TThO.	476	
1/26pm	Manchester Ex.	1/55	TThO.		ECS
2/00	Ordsall Lane	6/30	TThO.		ECS
6/35	Manchester Ex.	7/11	TThO.		
8/50	Chester.				
	Bangor	6.40am	SO.		ECS
7.06am	Caernarvon	7.15	SO.	52	
8.33	Llandudno	10 25	SO.	248	
1/43pm	Manchester Ex.	1/55pm	SO.		ECS
2/00	Ordsall Lane	6/30	SO.		ECS
6/35	Manchester Ex.	7/11	SO.		
8/50	Chester.				

Alternates with set 235.

Circuit Set 1220

3-coach Lavatory set. non-corridor.

arr.	Station	dep.	days	Rep.No.
	Bangor	4.51am	MWFO.	
6.10am	Afonwen	6.40	MWFO.	114
7.55	Bangor	8.20	MWFO.	58
11.15	Manchester Ex.	11.45	MWFO.	461
3/08pm	Llandudno	4/40pm	MWFO.	246
6/49	Chester	7/55	MWFO.	48
9/14	Liverpool L.St.			
	Liverpool L.St.	7.40am	TThO.	61
11.16am	Bangor	12/20pm	TThO.	
1/40pm	Afonwen	3/50	TThO.	
5/16	Bangor	5/40	TThO.	162
6/15	Llandudno Jn.	7/20	TThO.	127
7/56	Bangor	8/05	TThO.	
9/23	Afonwen	9/45	TThO.	
11/07	Bangor.			
	Liverpool L.St.	7.40am	SO.	61
11.16am	Bangor	12/20pm	SO.	
1/40pm	Afonwen	3/58	SO.	
5/25	Bangor	5/40	SO.	162
6/15	Llandudno Jn.	7/20	SO.	127
7/56	Bangor	8/05	SO.	
9/23	Afonwen	9/45	SO.	
11/07	Bangor.			

Alternates with set 1235.

As before, traffic sets kept to their home districts and usually worked one, two or three day circuits. Provision was also made to enable a train formation to be strengthened at short notice by spare coaches located at strategic stations, subject to Control approval and that the train's motive power was adequate. These spare coaches were also allocated circuit numbers. After 1950, some non-corridor sets were replaced by Inter-Corridor 3-coach sets. These were to be found working most of the Afonwen line traffic after that date, but the Amlwch line sets were still worked with non-corridor coaches. The advent of the DMU workings in 1956 saw the Amlwch service and initially one or two trips over the Afonwen line succumbed to this form of traction. The units were based at Llandudno Junction, although Bangor men continued to work over their own territory. Gradually though the Afonwen line succumbed to the all-conquering diesel for the winter services with units parked overnight at Bangor on the Down side carriage line. The Afonwen service reverted to steam hauled stock for the summer months with coaches working through to Manchester Exchange and Liverpool Lime Street, as before. The Class "A" stock from Pwllheli and Portmadoc to Euston working as The Welshman remained steam hauled until the last summer of operation. With the commencement of the winter schedules on 7th September 1964, only the 5.20am Bangor to Pwllheli (2J81) and the corresponding 2D81 7.45am Pwllheli to Bangor was hauled by steam. Steam hauled freight services disappeared from the working timetable beyond Caernarvon during the currency of the winter 1963 services.

One interesting factor which perhaps is of relevance to the modeller, was the appearance of rolling stock belonging to Regions other than the London Midland, at Bangor. Few 'foreign' workings were seen before nationalisation, but from 1948 to 1964 a variety of other region stock workings were to be seen with Western Region stock being the most common. One Bangor coach set incorporated a GWR corridor brake third, still in GWR colours, and which ran over the Afonwen line for several months in 1950. The various Butlins Specials regularly had through workings of LNER corridor stock from and to Huddersfield and Sheffield on Summer Saturdays. Neither was the Southern Region excluded, but only seen on rare occasions. I recall two successive Summer Saturdays in 1949 and 1950, when two

coaches of Bullied stock, resplendent in malachite green were found in a working from Warrington to Penychain. The period was the last week-end in July and the first week-end in August in each case, which was the Bank Holiday week-end at that time. Enquiries revealed that these coaches had been attached at Chester to strengthen an eight coach working that was packed to the rooftops. It was understood that the coaches had arrived off the Margate or Ramsgate to Birkenhead working the previous evening and were commandeered to ease the pressure on Chester platform, which was seething with humanity. They were attached to the front of the train, making the load up to 10, and stood out amongst the crimson and blood and custard stock at Bangor. The vehicles worked to Pwllheli East where the locos ran around the stock and worked back ECS to Bangor. 7B men and machines were replaced by a Chester Class 5 and a Warrington crew. The following Saturday saw a similar pair of coaches on the same working. They failed to appear after that and it was assumed that LM Region had been found its own stock for the working. However, the following year saw the same procedure, with the coaches still in malachite green. There was less maroon and more blood and custard on the coaching stock, and providing a splash of colour amongst the monotonous collection on hand. The workings were exactly the same as the previous year.

Robin Addey noted a report in a publication, sometime between 1953 and 1958, that a train of two five-coach sets of Southern Region stock worked to Bangor one Saturday, where the stock was split. One set worked through to Afonwen on the 11.12am working, whilst the second set worked back to Liverpool Lime Street. Of significance was the fact that the circuit numbers were recorded and given as Sets 427 and 432. These were allocated to Southern Region - Western & Southern Districts at this time.

No.74. Menai Bridge. 1964. In that final summer of passenger working over the Afonwen and Amlwch lines, steam power made a belated return to the latter branch, and a two coach push-pull set worked all the services after eight years of DMU operation. Here the 11.40am from Bangor pauses at the first stop, the driver comfortably placed in his cab, with inevitable brew can and cup on the front window ledge, newspaper visible in the centre window and a homeward bound ganger for company. At the tail end, an eruption of steam encompassing the 84XXX class 2-6-2T locomotive suggests that the injector has blown back. Beyond can be seen the signal box on the Caernarvon side, somewhat in need of a coat of paint. Apart from the traincrew, there is not much sign of life!   *Norman Kneale.*

No.75. Bangor (East End). c.1964. Duchess Class Pacific No.**46251** *City of Nottingham* of Crewe North shed (5A), takes the centre road through Bangor with the mid-day (SX) stock working 3A34 from Holyhead to Willesden. The working normally pulled into platform 1 for the twenty seven minute wait, but may have been routed on the centre road for an operating reason. Certainly it was not due to depart for another eight minutes, judging by the clock on the Down platform, so perhaps some shunting was taking place at the time of the photograph. An injector is blowing back under the fireman's side of the cab possibly caused by regulator closure. On the Down platform, vans are being unloaded during a quiet period between passenger services.

Norman Kneale.

No.76. Bangor (East End). 1963. Class 5 4-6-0 No.**44916** of Longsight Shed (9A) stands at the Up platform with the 6.55pm to Crewe, whilst No.**44682** of Chester Shed (6A) storms through the Up fast line under clear signals with a perishable special from Holyhead to Broad Street. On the Down platform, a DMU stands waiting to depart with the 7/12pm to Afonwen. Note the square post Lower Quadrant signals at the Down platform ramp, with the bottom arm being the calling-on signal for setting back movements. Just to the left of the signal post can be seen the Bethesda Bay starter, another square post lower quadrant fixture. These signals contrast with the modern upper quadrant arms on the tubular Up bracket projecting over the track.

Norman Kneale.

No.77. Bangor. 1964. Tank engines were an integral part of Bangor working, and the summer months saw the shed compliment almost doubled, Ivatt Class 2MT 2-6-2T No.**41226** stands at the Down platform with the 12.45pm Rail Motor to Amlwch. Further down the platform, Stanier design Class 4 2-6-4T No.**42488** slowly draws up the platform with the 12.45pm for Pwllheli. The 10.45am Portmadoc to Manchester (reporting number 1C77) runs into the Up platform, hauled by Stanier Class 2-6-4T No.**42478** and piloted by Fairburn 2-6-4T No.**42074**.

Norman Kneale.

No.78. Bangor (Down Loop Platform). August 1962. Stanier Jubilee Class 4-6-0 No.**45652** *Hawke*, carrying a Warrington (8B) shedplate on the smokebox door, and sporting Class 1 headlamps pauses at the eastern end of the Down passenger Loop on its journey through the platform road. Warrington was not normally associated with Class 6 passenger locomotive turns. A collection of lamps rest in the six foot by the ground disk signal.

Norman Kneale.

No.79. Bangor (Up Platform). April 1963. Princess Coronation Class Pacific No.**46225** *Duchess of Gloucester* stands at the Up platform with a Holyhead to Crewe working. Several of these locomotives were painted in a maroon livery, which suited their massive bulk, although the remainder of the class were in B.R. lined green livery whilst the author has fond memories of working on this engine when it sported the short lived Blue livery. One of the reasons given for the variation was that the locomotives in red were generally to be seen on daytime duties, such as the prestige 'Caledonian' working between Euston and Glasgow, when the public would appreciate the uniform colour with the rolling stock, whilst the ones that generally worked overnight duties were to be left in green, on the assumption that the public would be less likely to notice such detail during the hours of darkness. Whatever the truth of the issue, it mattered little to the men who worked these engines, whose main concern was to have a good sound machine with which to perform their duty. This particular duty was the return working of a Crewe North diagram, which was normally the province of a Class 6 working, and as already mentioned, 46225 was allocated to Carlisle Upperby (12A) at the time of this photograph. During the week, the train ran as Reporting Number 1K83 as far as Chester, when it changed its Reporting Number to 2K56, and stopped at Tattenhall Road as well as Beeston Castle, for which it was allowed an extra two minutes on the Saturday Only schedule. Thirty eight minutes for the 21 miles hardly taxed the engine or men.

Norman Kneale.

No. 80. Bangor (Up Passenger Loop). 1964. Rebuilt Royal Scot Class 4-6-0 No.**46152** *The King's Dragoon Guardsman* of Holyhead Shed (6J) stands at the Up Passenger Loop platform with a Class 1 Passenger working for Crewe whilst its successor stands in the Up platform. Caernarvon Road passed under the tracks at this point. When the station was enlarged in 1924 the Up Passenger and Goods Loop Lines were added, necessitating bridging the road a second time. The enclosing wall provided a safety barrier. Note also the usual lineside furniture in the foreground.

B.A. Wynne.

No.81. Bangor (East End). 1964. Rebuilt Patriot Class 4-6-0 No.**45527** *Southport* pulls away from Bangor with a Crewe working in the last summer of its life. The diagonal stripe across the cab sides dates the photograph, and the locomotive was nominally attached to Carlisle Upperby (12B) although steam locomotive diagrams were interpreted quite freely, and were pressed into service on workings as needs demanded. This turn was a Crewe North diagram on certain days during the week and it is believed that 5A men were in control on this occasion. These rebuilt Patriots were excellent machines, and were put to the scrap heap with plenty of life remaining in them. *Norman Kneale.*

No.82. Bangor (East End). June 1964. Fairburn Class 4MT 2-6-4T No.**42236** of Chester Shed (6A) pulls away from Bangor with the 3.50pm Chester. These tank engine were fully up to the demands of the job, and could run at speeds up to 80mph with ease. Some of the class were fitted with water pick-up apparatus, which avoided the need for a lengthy wait at a platform column en route. Notice the ornamental tunnel mouth, and the suspended bracket signals for the Down line. Sighting of these signals was sometimes difficult, particularly if another train had passed through the tunnel recently. *Norman Kneale.*

No.83 Bangor. 1947. As mentioned elsewhere, Bangor station was confined geographically. The course of the line crossing a shallow valley, and rail access was through tunnels at either end of the complex. At the eastern end, the tunnel burrowed through Bangor mountain and was appropriately named. It was dead straight, on a gentle gradient, and at times the opposite tunnel mouth could be seen. It is 914 yards in length and brick lined throughout. The western end of the tunnel portal was faced in the 'Egyptian' style, to complement the Britannia Tubular bridge. A signal gantry stood at the tunnel mouth on the Down side, but smoke usually inhibited sighting of the signals, and caution was exercised by trains calling at the station.   *J.M. Dunn.*

No.84. Bangor. August 1963. A batch of five, equipped with Caprotti valve gear went into traffic at Crewe or Llandudno Junction, between 26th May and 19th June 1948 and all were allocated to 7A shed by 28th June. They took over most of the workings between Crewe, Llandudno and Manchester. Four remained at the Junction until 1960 or later. Here No.**44739**, seen pulling away from the Up Loop platform remained at Llandudno Junction until 9th November 1963 when it transferred to Speke Junction.   *T. Lewis.*

No.85. Bangor (Motive Power Yard). 14th August 1954. Brand-new Britannia Class Pacific No.70050 without shed or name plates, stands on No.2 shed road whilst the traincrew pose for the Locomotive Shedmaster, J.M. Dunn, who took this photograph. It was being prepared for the second part of "The Welshman",W100B   *J.M. Dunn.*

Working Arrangements

The Rostered Turns for the summer period commencing July 8th 1929 showed the following make-up of the duties.

PASSENGER ENGINES

Turn No.	Loco Type	Work (Pass unless stated)	Days
Turn 1	Claughton	Bangor-Euston	MWFO
		Euston-Bangor	TThSO
Turn 2	Claughton	Bangor-Euston	MWFO
		Euston-Bangor	TThSO
Turn 3	Geo V.	Bangor-Manchester-Bangor	FSX
		Bangor-Manchester	FO
		Manchester-Bangor	SO
Turn 4	Geo.V.	Bangor-Holyhead-Llan.Jn.-Bangor	D
		Bangor-Chester-Bangor	D
Turn 5	Geo.V.	Bangor-Chester-Bangor	SX
		Bangor-Lime St.-Bangor	SO
Turn 6	Geo.V.	Bangor-Chester-Bangor	D
Turn 7	Claughton	Bangor-Euston	FO
		Euston-Llandudno-Bangor	SO
Turn 8	Geo.V.	Bangor-Manchester-Bangor	SO
Turn 9	Geo.V.	Bangor-Manchester-Bangor	SO
Turn 10	Geo.V.	Bangor-Chester-Bangor	MO
		Bangor-Manchester-Bangor	SO
Turn 11	Geo.V.	Bangor-Manchester-Bangor	SO
Turn 12	Coal Tank	Bangor-Llandudno-Bangor	SX
		Bangor-Llandudno-Llanberis-Bangor	SO
Turn 13	18" 0-6-0	Bangor-Afonwen-Bangor (Frt/Pass)	D
		Bangor-Afonwen-Bangor (Pass/Frt)	D
Turn 14	18" 0-6-0	Bangor-Afonwen-Bangor	D
		Bangor-Caernarvon-M.Br.-Bangor	D
Turn 15	4-6-2T	Bangor-Afonwen-Bangor	D
		Bangor-Afonwen-Bangor	D
Turn 16	Coal Tank	Bangor-Afonwen-Bangor (Frt/Pass)	D
		Bangor-Afonwen-Bangor	D
Turn 17	Coal Tank	Bangor-Afonwen-Bangor (Frt/Pass)	D
		Bangor-Afonwen-Bangor	D
Turn 18	4-6-2T	Bangor-Afonwen-Bangor	D
		Bangor-Afonwen-Bangor (Pass/Frt)	D
Turn 19	Coal Tank	Bangor-Afonwen-Bangor	D
		Bangor-Afonwen-Bangor	D
Turn 21	5' 6" 2-4-2T	Bangor-Red Wharf Bay-Gaerwen	D
		Gaerwen-Red Wharf Bay-Bangor	D

Turn 22	5' 6" 2-4-2T	Bangor-Red Wharf Bay-Bangor (Frt)	D
Turn 23	5' 6" 2-4-2T	Bangor-Amlwch-Bangor	D
		Bangor-Amlwch-Bangor	D
Turn 24	5' 6" 2-4-2T	Bangor-Amlwch-Bangor	D
		Bangor-Llangefni-Bangor	ThO
Turn 25	0-6-2T	Bangor-Bethesda-Bangor (6 trips)	D
		Bangor-Bethesda-Bangor (8 trips)	D
		Bangor-C/von-Llan.Jn-C/von-Bangor.	Sun

Note: (Frt/Pass) indicates Freight Working on outward trip and Passenger Working on inward journey.

FREIGHT ENGINES

Turn 1F	2x19" loco only	Menai Bridge-Crewe-Menai Bridge	D
Turn 2F	(men only)	Menai Bridge-Crewe	M-FO
		Crewe-Bangor	Tue-Sat
Turn 3F	R.O.D. 2-8-0	Bangor-Mold Jn.	Sun
		Mold Jn.-Bangor	MO
		Menai Bridge-Mold Jn	MTO
		Mold Jn.-Holyhead-M.Br.-Bangor	TWO
Turn 4F	2xR.O.D. 2-8-0	Bangor-Penm'mawr-Mold Jn.-M.Br.	D
Turn 5F	Coal Tank	Bangor-Bethesda-Bangor (Frt)	SO
Turn 6F	Coal Tank	Menai Bridge Shunt	SX
Turn 7F	Coal Tank	Bangor-Bethesda-Port Siding-Bangor	SX
		Bangor-Port Penrhyn-Bangor	MWFO
Turn 8F	18" 0-6-0	Bangor-Holyhead-Bangor (Frt)	D
		Bangor-Valley-Bangor (Frt)	D
Turn 9F	Cl.4F 0-6-0	Menai Bridge Shunt	TThSO
Turn 10F	(9F engine)	Bangor-Port Penrhyn-Bangor	MWFO
Turn 11F	Coal Engine	Bangor-Port Siding-Bangor	D
Turn 12F	Coal Engine	Bangor-Menai Bridge-Bangor	SX
Turn 13F		SPARE	
Turn 15F		SPARE	
Turn 16F	Coal Engine	Bangor Freight Shunt (2 sets men)	D
Turn 17F	Men only	Preparation Set	SO

PASSENGER ENGINE WORKINGS IN DETAIL

Turn 1 Class 5 Engine (Claughton)

	Bangor	8.35am	MWFO	Pass
9.50am	Chester	10.00	MWFO	
10.27	Crewe	10.35	MWFO	
1/25pm	Euston	-		
-	Camden			
	Book Off			
	Camden	-	TThO	LE
-	Euston	10.40am	TThO	Pass
2/29pm	Crewe	2/36pm	TThO	
3/06	Chester	3/27	TThO	
4/49	Bangor			
	Camden	-	SO	LE
-	Euston	10.40am	SO	Pass
2/29pm	Crewe	2/36pm	SO	
3/06	Chester	3/27	SO	
4/49	Bangor			

Turn 2 Class 5 Engine (Claughton)

	Bangor	11.55am	MWFO	Pass
4/57pm	Euston	-	MWFO	
-	Camden			
	Book Off			
	Camden	-	TThSO	LE
-	Euston	11.10am	TThSO	Pass
4/06pm	Bangor			

In 1939 The Number 1 Link comprised 4 sets of men for the winter workings and 6 sets in the summer duties.

The Winter Work was as follows:

Monday	Tuesday	Wednesday	Thursday	Friday	Saturday	Sunday
Euston 8.08am	Bangor 10.40am	H'head 7.45am	H'head 7.45am	H'head 7.45am	H'head 7.45am	-
H'head 7.45am	H'head 7.45am	Llan.Jn 3/50pm	Llan.Jn. 3/50pm	L'pool 12/17pm	Crewe 8.10am	Bangor 3.15am
-	-	Euston 8.33am	Bangor 10.40am	Euston 8.33am	Bangor 10.40am	-
L'pool 12/17pm	L'pool 12/17pm	L'pool 12/17pm	L'pool 12/17pm	-	L'pool 11.17am	-

The 8.10am to Crewe was a lodging turn.

Summer Duties were:

Monday	Tuesday	Wednesday	Thursday	Friday	Saturday	Sunday
H'head 7.45am		Euston 8.33am	Bangor 10.40am	Euston 8.33am	Bangor 10.40am	-
Chester 3/15pm	Chester 3/15pm	Chester 3/15pm	Cheste 3/15pm	M'chester 3/15pm	Afonwen 11.15am	-
Euston 8.33am	Bangor 10.40am	-	-	Euston 10.30am	Colwyn Bay 11.05am	-
Rhyl 5/05pm	Rhyl 5/05pm	Rhyl 5/05pm	Rhyl 5/05pm	Rhyl 5/05pm	M'nchester 12/40pm	-
Euston 10.30am	Bangor 11.15am	Euston 10.30am	Bangor 11.15am		M'chester 10.35am	-
Chester 12/40pm	Chester 12/40pm	Chester 12/40pm	Chester 12/40pm	Chester 12/40pm	Liverpool 10.35am	-

No.2. Link had a lodging turn to Manchester on Fridays during the summer workings. The job left Bangor at 1/40pm for Chester, where the crew changed footplates and took over a Class 4 2-6-4T and worked the 4/00pm local to Warrington. They then worked the 5/15pm to Wigan and worked Empty Stock via Tyldesley to Patricroft where they booked off. The next morning they worked the 11.15am from Manchester Exchange to Afonwen as far as Bangor.

In September 1944 The composition of the Link Structure for Footplate Staff was as follows:

No.1. Link	6 sets.	1 Sunday Turn
No.2. Link	9 sets.	1 Sunday Turn
No.3. Link	10 sets.	2 Sunday Turns
No.4. Link	5 sets.	1 Sunday Turn
No.5. Link.	9 sets.	
No.6. Link.	9 sets.	
No.7. Link.	3 sets.	(Shed Turning).

The Working Arrangements for the period commencing 16th June 1947 was as follows:

Rostered Turns:

Turn	Days	Work	Type
25	Mon-Sat	6.20am Llanberis	Goods
27	Mon-Sat	7.40am Llandudno Junction	Pass
28	Tue-Sat	2/05pm Llandudno	Freight
29	Sat	8.15am Afonwen	Freight
30	Sat	1/55pm Afonwen & Chwilog	Pass
32	Mon-Sat	9/25pm Bangor-Broad Green	Milk. L/T
33	Tue-Sat	3/05pm Broad Green-Bangor	Milk Eties
34	Sun	3/15pm Broad Green-Bangor	Milk Eties
35	Sun	4/50pm Chwilog-Broad Green	Milk L/T
36	Mon	3/05pm Broad Green-Bangor	Milk Eties
37	Mon-Sat	5.05am Amlwch	Mail
38	Mon-Sat	12/25pm Amlwch	Pass
40	Mon-Fri	10.48am Llanfair	Freight
47	Mon	6.55am Afonwen	Milk Eties
48	Mon-Fri	3/55pm Amlwch	Pass
49	Mon-Sat	6.25am Amlwch	Pass
50	Mon-Fri	12/25pm Menai Bridge	Shunt
52	Mon-Sat	7.25am Bethesda	Motor
53	Mon-Sat	3/00pm Bethesda	Motor
54	Sat	7.30am P.Way Engineers	Dept.
55	Sat	7.30am P.Way Engineers (Oct.4th only)	Dept.
56	Sun	3.15am Crewe (Short Rest)	Pass
57	Sun }	7.35am Crewe (Lodging Turn)	Pass L/T
58	Sun }	8/25pm Crewe-Chester, 11/55 Bangor	Pass
59	Mon-Fri	9.00am Penygroes	Pass
60	Mon-Fri	7.30am Penygroes	Goods
61	Mon-Sat	6.10am Caernarvon	L.E.
62	Tue-Sat	3.40am Caernarvon	Goods
63	Mon-Sat	12/40pm (SX) 7.35am (SO) Freight	Shunt
65	Mon-Sat	4.46am Afonwen	Pass
66	Tue-Sat	7.30am Holyhead	Pass
67	Mon-Fri	9.10am Holyhead	Pass
68	Mon-Fri	12/35pm Afonwen	Freight
71	Mon-Fri	2/45pm Afonwen	Pass
72	Sat	3/05pm Afonwen	Pass
73	Mon-Fri	10.00am Afonwen	Pass
75	Mon-Fri	11.15am Freight	Shunt
76	Mon-Sat	12/20pm Afonwen	Pass
77	Mon-Fri	1/40pm Llan.Jn.	Pass
77	Sat	1/40pm Llan.Jn.+ 4/35pm Afonwen	Pass
78	Mon-Sat	5.45am Afonwen	Pass
79	Mon-Thu	3/45pm Chester	Pass
80	Sat	3/45pm Chester	Pass
81	Mon-Fri	5/30pm Llandudno Junction	Pass
82	Mon-Fri	5/40pm Llandudno Junction	Pass
85	Tue	3/45pm Holyhead	Pass
86	Sat	5/35pm Afonwen	Pass
87	Sat	7.35am Afonwen	L.E.
88	Sat	1/55pm Afonwen	Pass
89	Sat	8.15am Afonwen	L.E.
90	Sat	4/05pm Afonwen	Pass
91	Sat	4/05pm Afonwen	Cpld
92	Sat	3/55pm Amlwch	Pass
93	Sat	9.45am Caernarvon	ECS
94	Mon-Sat	4.46am	Passenger Shunt
95	Mon-Sat	2/15pm Caernarvon	Shunt
96	Mon	4.30am	
97	Mon-Fri	4/20pm Colwyn Bay	Pass
99	Mon-Sat	6.45am Llandudno Junction	Pass
100	Mon-Sat	6.55am Holyhead	Pass
101	Mon-Fri	2/45pm Llandudno Junction	Pass
108	Tue	8.20am Chester (P.Way)	Dept.
110	Mon-Fri	7.35am Shunt + Bethesda	Freight
111	Sat	9.10am Holyhead-Chester	Pass

Rostered Turns (continued)

112	Mon	7.30am Holyhead	Pass
113	Fri	3/45pm Holyhead (as pass)-Llan.Jn.	Freight
115	Sat	11.15am Passenger Station	Shunt
116	Sat	8.30am Caernarvon	Freight
140	Mon-Fri	2.55am Menai Bridge Shunt	Trip
141	Mon-Fri	9.00am Port Penrhyn Shunt	Trip
142	Sat	2.55am Menai Bridge Shunt	Trip
143	Sat	12/25pm Menai Bridge Shunt	Trip
144	Mon-Fri	10.50am Port Siding	Freight
145	Mon-Fri	6/00pm Menai Bridge Shunt	Trip
149	MWFO	9.40am Red Wharf Bay	Freight
150	Mon	12.25am Menai Bridge Shunt	Trip
151	Mon-Fri	8.50am Amlwch	Freight
153	Mon-Sat	5.15am Bangor Goods Yard	Shunt
156	Mon-Fri	12/25pm Amlwch	Freight
157	Sat	8.50am Amlwch	Freight
161	Mon-Fri}	{ 2/50pm Menai Bridge to Mold Junct	Freight
162	Tue-Sat}	{ 7.30am Mold Junction to Bangor	Freight
165	Sat	2/45pm M.Bridge Relieve 6.50am M.Jn.	Freight
166	Mon-Fri	10/55pm Llan.Jn. Relieve 1.21am M.Jn	Freight
171	Sat	2/50pm Mold Junction	Freight
172	Mon-Sat	12/55pm (SX) 2/50pm (SO) Llan.Jn.	Freight
178	Mon-Fri	7/20pm Menai Bridge to Llandudno Jn.	Freight
180	Sat	11.45am Caernarvon (as passenger)	Shunt
190	Mon-Sat	6.00am Turning	
190	Mon-Sat	2/00pm Turning	
190	Mon-Sat	10/00pm Turning	
190	Mon	12.01am Turning	
190	Sun	6.00am Turning	
190	Sun	2/00pm Turning.	

The Link Structure for the same period was as follows:

No.1. Link. 8 sets.

Sun	Mon	Tue	Wed	Thu	Fri	Sat
57	101	101	101	101	101	
	113	66	66	66	66	66
	68	68	68	68	68	109
34	67	67	67	67	67	111
	112	112	112	112	112	55
	61	61	61	61	61	61
	79	79	79	79	79	79
	65	65	65	65	65	65

No.2. Link. 10 sets.

Sun	Mon	Tue	Wed	Thu	Fri	Sat
	60	60	60	59	60	60
	178	178	178	178	82	165
	73	100	100	100	100	100
	76	76	76	76	76	76
	33	33	33	33	33	33
150+166	166	166	166	166		
	78	78	78	78	78	78
	161	162	161	162	161	162
	35	35	35	35	35	35
	81	81	81	81	81	77

Note that traincrew working Turn 150 on Monday morning
also worked Turn 166 the same evening

No.3. Link. 10 sets.

Sun	Mon	Tue	Wed	Thu	Fri	Sat
	96	62	62	62	62	62
	42	43	42	43	42	43
	100	73	73	73	73	73
	97	97	97	97	97	190
	110	110	110	110	110	111
	43	42	43	42	43	171
	149	174	149	174	149	
	34	34	34	34	34	34
	156	59	59	60	59	59
	59	156	156	156	156	

No.4. Link. 6 Sets.

Sun	Mon	Tue	Wed	Thu	Fri	Sat
	37	37	37	37	37	37
	53	53	53	53	53	53
	52	52	52	52	52	52
	77	77	77	77	77	
	151	151	151	151	151	151
	38	38	38	38	38	38

No.5. Link. 7 Sets.

Sun	Mon	Tue	Wed	Thu	Fri	Sat
	99	99	99	99	99	99
	71	71	71	71	71	72
	50	50	50	50	50	50
	48	161	162	161	162	42
	82	82	82	82	178	54
	144	108	144	Spare	148	143
	49	49	49	49	49	92

No.6. Link. 10 Sets.

Sun	Mon	Tue	Wed	Thu	Fri	Sat
	140	140	140	140	140	142
	95	95	95	95	95	180
	141	141	141	141	141	174
	179	179	179	179	179	83
	94	94	94	94	94	94
	51	51	51	51	51	114
	63	63	63	63	63	63
	152	152	152	152	152	153
	75	75	75	75	75	115
	172	172	172	172	172	172

No.7. Link. 3 Sets. (Turning Link).

Sun	Mon	Tue	Wed	Thu	Fri	Sat
	6.00	6.00	6.00	6.00	6.00	6.00
	2/00	2/00	2/00	2/00	2/00	2/00
	12.01}					
	10/00}	10/00	10/00	10/00	10/00	-

Note that the traincrew working 12.01am turn on Monday
Morning also worked the 10/00pm shift the same evening.

LOCOMOTIVE DEPARTMENT MISCELLANY

The Officers in Charge of Bangor Shed over the years were:

J. Sellars	1880 to -	
? Godber	- to 1901	
G. Dingley	1901 to 1904	Died "in harness" aged 36
F.A. Lemon	1906	Works Manager at Crewe
C.E. Winby	1906 to 1911	
J. Geffert	1911	Sacked after Royal Train fiasco
N.B. Richards	1912 to 1913	
G.H. Nelson	1913	
?. Aylmer	1913	
H. Nevitt	1915 to 1917	
W.H. Power	to 1920	Left Railway Service.
H.K. Bostock	1920 to 1926	
A. Dingley	1926 to 1932	
A. Broxton	1932	Died before taking up post.
H. Edwards	1932 to 1940	
A. Webb	1940 to 1944	
G.W. Fraser	1944	Acting R.S.Foreman.
J.M. Dunn	1944 to 1958	
A. Stone	1958 to	Mechanical Inspector Chester
D.L. Jones	to 1965	Shed closed 12:06:65.

Chief Clerks at Bangor Shed.

?. Skelly	to 1897
J. Bates	1897 to 1931
B.J. Vaughan	1931 to 1946
A.W. Western	1946
E.J. Parry	1946 to 1953
R.G. Morris	1953 to 1961
?. Hanson	1961 to

The first Locomotive Departmental Committee meeting was held at the shed on 4th September 1922 at 2/30pm.

On 24th February 1933, the district succumbed to a snow storm and three Bangor engines were stranded at Afonwen. The men were on duty for 34, 35 and 36 hours respectively.

On 28th February 1935, two ex Lancashire & Yorkshire 2-4-2 Class 2PT engines were working on the Amlwch and Afonwen lines. They were not very successful and the reserve of water when working with 63 tons to Amlwch was very small. No engine numbers were stated.

On 30th November of the same year, S.T.C. engines Nos 7729 and 27669 broke their main frame through the trailing coupled horn-gap.

The following January saw an entry that the shed doors have been damaged and there was now little use for them!

On 29th July the Class 3PT 2-6-2 engines were not able to keep time with a full load and requested that the loading was altered. This was obviously done and the next entry, dated 31st August stated the same engines were reported doing good work with a fair load.

On 27th February 1937 the pit in the coal stage had been filled in and re-laid with sleepered road. By 30th October that year Nos. 5 and 6 shed road pits were concreted.

On Christmas Eve, there was an unspecified mishap to a passenger train in Bangor station. Just over a month later, on 31st January 1938, the Great Western Railway turntable at Afonwen had been removed.

The Emergency Time Tables came into force on 11th September 1939. Three trains per day to Afonwen comprised the total service beyond Caernarfon, with two additional trains between Bangor and Caernarfon on weekdays, and another three on Saturdays. Amlwch branch had four trains daily for the same period. The service improved early in 1940 when conditions were relaxed.

A new centre-pin was fitted to the turntable on Sunday 8th September 1940.

J.M. Dunn took up the appointment as Running Shed Foreman on 4th September 1944.

No. 86 Menai Bridge. April 1955. A careers visit for schoolboys was arranged to inspect the Britannia Tubular Bridge, involving a special 'stop in section' to set the passengers down. Ivatt 2-6-2T No. 41324, then based at Bangor Shed (6H) was the motive power, and the vehicle used was the LNWR built District Engineer's Saloon. Departmental number 45012. The Chief Civil Engineer's Personal Assistant, Mr Fergus Wilson is seen standing to the right of the steps. On the extreme right hand side can be seen Mr Ronny Waugh, Assistant District Engineer to Mr Cunningham based at Bangor.

M.S. Welch

Engines & Men.

No.87. Bangor. Motive Power yard. Early 1960's. Ifor Roberts (standing) waits to swing the water column arm back to rest whilst Norman Jones perches on the tender top of Class 5 4-6-0 No.**45145**, keeping an eye on the rising water level.

Norman Kneale.

No.88. Bangor Motive Power Yard. c.1963. From left to right, Harold Bargh, (Coalman); Griffith Williams (Guto Bach) Fireman and Driver Zacariah (Zac) Owen pose for the photographer alongside BR Standard Class 2 2-6-2 No.**84009.** Note the Eastern Region coach in the carriage siding road. *Norman Kneale*

No.89. Holyhead Motive Power Yard. c.1963. Driver Aled Hughes and an unknown Fireman stand on the 70ft turntable at Holyhead with Class 5 No.**45426** of 5A prior to working back to Bangor. Notice the turntable motor vacuum hose connected to the leading vacuum pipe on the front bufferbeam. The driver would blow off the brakes and the vacuum created was used to turn the locomotive. *Norman Kneale.*

No.90. Bangor Motive Power Yard. c.1963. Class 5 4-6-0 No.**45345** forms the backdrop as R.H. Owen (Fitter); Ieuan Hughes, (Fireman); J.O. Jones (Steamraiser) and Richard Davies (Driver) pose for the photographer. *Norman Kneale.*

No.91. Bangor, c.1963. Driver Sydney Kelly and Fireman Wil Williams (Amlwch) put on cheerful faces for the photographer. The loco, Ivatt Class 2 2-6-2T No.**41200** is in very dirty state, the windows and even the number obscured by accumulated grime. *Norman Kneale.*

No.92. Bangor Motive Power Yard. c.1963. Ensuring the locomotives were in safe working condition was the responsibility of the Repaired Engines Staff. Here 'Mac' Thompson, one of Bangor's fitters poses, hammer in one hand and pipe in mouth, alongside Ivatt 2-6-2T No.**41287**. *Norman Kneale.*

No.93. Bangor Goods Yard. c.1963. The shunter rarely attracted the attention of photographers, although they performed an essential service usually in very difficult conditions. Here John Williams (Jack Bach) wields his pole between two vans whilst keeping an eye on the camera. *Norman Kneale.*

No.94. Bangor Station. East End. c.1963. Britannia Class Pacific No.**70051** *Firth of Forth* sets back on the Up Fast line under the careful scrutiny of Signalman Arthur Peglar from No.1 signal box. *Norman Kneale.*

No.95. Bangor. West End. c.1964. Britannia Class Pacific No.**70047**, the only engine in the class not to be named, stands on the Down platform line with a Holyhead working. Driver Norman Jones and Fireman Brian G. Williams watch the cameraman prior to moving off. Note the bracket for the driver's name badge below the window - rarely if ever used. *Norman Kneale.*

No.96.(top left) **Bangor Motive Power Yard. c.1964.** Surrounded by piles of ash discarded from fireboxes, Fireman Derwyn Williams prepares for duty, black jacket over his arm, in front of one of the depot's 2-6-2T engines which was fitted for push pull working. **No.97.**(bottom left) The Repaired Engines staff were rarely seen, and probably preferred to keep a low profile. However Fitters Robert H. Owen (Bob Meth.) and Maldwyn Morris (Moi Fitter) stand between two of the Depots stud of tank engines with tools in evidence. **No.98.**(top right) The first requirement for staff in all grades when coming on duty was to sign on. Here in somewhat cramped but typical conditions, are John Roberts (Jack Blackpool), Labourer; Moi Edwards of Caernarfon (Driver); Robert Humphries (Passed Fireman) with John Williams (Passed Fireman) at the window. **No.99.** (centre right) Driver Dick Jones and Fireman Hugh Williams stand by their locomotive for their photograph, one cold day. Not every driver wore the regulation headgear. **No.100.** (bottom right) Just as essential as drivers and firemen in any depot were the inside men, like Richard Williams (Labourer); Robert Evan Roberts (Foreman's Assistant) and Robert Hughes (Storeman). It is pleasing to place on record the invaluable contribution these gentlemen played in the smooth running of Bangor depot.

all: Norman Kneale.

No.101. Bangor Motive Power Yard. c.1964. Class 5 4-6-0 No.**45247** stands on No.5 road receiving extra special treatment and attention to prepare it for working a Royal Train. Notice the warning target hanging on the smokebox door. Fireman Errol Davies (Knock-out!) stands alongside Driver Norman Jones (Llangefni) whilst the Foreman Cleaner John Williams (Jack Bradley) surveys the scene. Note the piles of ash littering the shed yard.   *Norman Kneale.*

No.102. Bangor Motive Power Dept. c.1964. Standing 'dead' on No.5 shed road is Class 5 4-6-0 No.**45298** alongside Standard Class 2 No.**78058**. Driver Leslie Hughes sits on the front frame plate whilst Harold Bargh, Coalman; John Roberts (Jack Blackpool), Fire dropper; R.H. Owen, Fitter; Ted Roberts, Firedropper and Fireman J.O. Williams (John Stores) stand in front of the bufferbeam. Note the snow plough kept in readiness by the shed wall.   *Norman Kneale.*

No.103. Bangor Motive Power Yard. c.1962. Sunday mornings on any Motive Power depot saw most of its allocation 'at home', and rarely was there space to spare. Modern LMS designs predominate and steam is being raised in readiness for the exodus that would take place after midnight. The carriage sidings are similarly full, with coaching stock parked temporarily on the Down Goods Loop alongside the shed wall, as well as on the Carriage Siding road, and in the stock sidings to the left of the picture. *Norman Kneale.*

No.104. Bangor Motive Power Depot. 1965. Perhaps there is nothing more depressing than the interior of a Motive Power Depot after it has closed to traffic and the locomotives transferred away. Some idea of the expanse of even small sheds like Bangor, with six inside roads, was rarely recorded. No.6 road is host to a few wagons, but all the stores that once lined the shed walls have been removed, apart from an odd oil drum. In the far end of the yard can be seen the 'gonging off' hut, with the tracks converging on Belmont tunnel. Perhaps Bangor is more fortunate in that the shed buildings were not demolished but became the premises for Stockwells, the Steel Stockholder, who constructed an extension at the open end of the shed, enclosing the building but which also preserved it. Perhaps in the future it might revert to its proper function and house steam locomotives again? *Norman Kneale.*

No.105. Bangor Motive Power Yard. 5th May 1957. Two Fowler 2-6-4T locomotives, No.**42356** of Stoke shed, coupled to No.**42366** of Macclesfield shed top up their tanks prior to working a Railtour Special to Bethesda and other branch lines. Notice the two styles of crest on the tank sides. The 2-6-4T engines were no strangers to Bangor, the normal allocation from 1948 until the last few months of the shed's existence varying from 12 to 14, depending on the time of the year, with the Fowler open cab variety perhaps the exception.   *Derek J. Lowe.*

No.106. Bangor Motive Power Yard. 9th July 1953. Following her Coronation the Queen toured North Wales on 10th July 1953. It fell to Bangor to work the Royal Train from its overnight resting place between Tal y Cafn and Glan Conway to Caernarfon. Two Class 4 2-6-4T engines were selected by the Running Shed Foreman and specially prepared for the event. The cleaning was given special attention, and the end result were these immaculate engines, Nos.**42455** and **42157**. The Staff worked with such enthusiasm that Commercial Photographers were commissioned to take three photographs by J.M. Dunn at his own expense, seen here with E. Parry, the Chief Clerk.   *Mark Radley & Co.*

No.107. Bangor. Belmont Tunnel. c.1963. Driver Eric Lynn and Fireman William Williams (Wil Amlwch), look back as they enter the tunnel with Fairburn 2-6-4T No.**42282** on an Afonwen working.
Norman Kneale.

No.109. Bangor. c.1964. Former Western Region 'Britannia' Class Pacific 4-6-2 No.**70024** *Vulcan* transferred to Crewe North in late 1963, and worked on the North Wales coast for a couple of years before moving north to Carlisle. Here, Fireman Aled Roberts sits at the controls whilst Driver S. Hughes stands by the cab door. The lack of cleaning is apparent, with the cab side number barely visible through the grime.
Norman Kneale.

No.108. Bangor Motive Power Yard. 1964. Fitter Tom Hughes pauses from his duties to look out of the cab of Royal Train engine, Class 5 No.**45247** as it stands just outside the shed entrance. *Norman Kneale.*

No.110. Bangor Down Platform. c.1963. Ivatt 2-6-2T No.**41226** takes water from the tank by the ramp of the Down platform. Driver Hugh Hughes (Minffordd) attends to the procedure, presumably his fireman is making up the fire. They already have the starter, and will depart for Menai Bridge when they are ready. *Norman Kneale.*

No.111. Bangor Motive Power Yard. 1964. Another Class 5 4-6-0 stands ready for its Royal Train duties. No.**44821** waits its turn of duty with a proud staff gathered alongside. Seen here are, from left to right, Pat Fitzpatrick, Boiler washer-out; Wil Williams (Amlwch), Cleaner; Tom Hughes, Fitter; R.H. Owen, Fitter; unknown; H.I. Owen, Fitters Mate; Jack ?, Fitters Mate. The three gentlemen on the right of the picture are, alas, unknown. *Norman Kneale.*

No.112. Bangor Motive Power Yard. August.1963. The two Royal Train engines, Class 5 4-6-0's Nos. **45247** and **45282** stand awaiting departure time prior to taking up their working. John Williams (Jack Bradley) the Foreman Cleaner walks over the tracks towards the locomotives, well proud of his staff and their efforts. *Norman Kneale.*

No.113. Bangor West End. August 1963. Class 5 4-6-0 No.**45247** accelerates towards Chester with the Royal Train engine, with Fitter Tom Hughes, Fireman Harold Blain, Driver David John Jones and an unknown fourth person on board. Since the regulations specified that a maximum of four persons should be on the footplate at any one time, just who is driving! *Norman Kneale.*

No.114. Bangor Motive Power Yard. Summer 1964. Class 5 4-6-0 No.**45422** of Shrewsbury (6D) Shed stands amidst piles of ash and clinker. The headcode 1D06 does not appear in the Working Time Table for the period, but the chalked number on the smokebox door 1M09 was the 9.10am Paddington to Birkenhead, worked by Shrewsbury men as far as Chester. Presumably the locomotive had been pressed into service on a special working.
Norman Kneale.

No.115. Bangor Motive Power Yard. c.1964. Jubilee Class 4-6-0 No.**45600** *Bermuda*, of Patricroft (9H) shed lurches on the track in the yard, which was perhaps not in tip top condition. The working number 1T51 indicated a train working from the Western Lines section into Central Lines, whilst the '51' suffix was similarly not listed, and was a spare number. The loco was taking up an extra train working.
Norman Kneale.

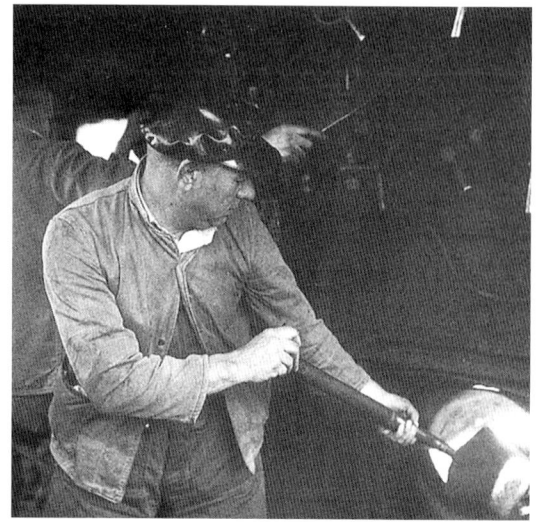

No.118. Bangor, c.1963. Somewhere on the line, fireman S.V. Jones, attends to the fire whilst driver Fred Morgan stands with right hand on the regulator and left hand on the small ejector handle of an unidentified Class 5 4-6-0. *Norman Kneale.*

No.116. Bangor Motive Power Yard. c.1964. On an unidentifiable class 5 4-6-0, from left to right, Thomas John Jones (Tos), Passed Fireman; Will Williams (Wil Amlwch), Fireman, stand in the cab, whilst at floor level, John Owen Jones, (Jack Stem), Steamraiser and Glyn Williams, Labourer, pose for the photographer. *Norman Kneale.*

No.119. Bangor Motive Power Yard. c.1963. Steam raiser John Ansonia sits at the fireman's window of Class 2 2-6-2T No.**41234** which was a long term resident at Bangor, from 1956 to 1965.

Norman Kneale.

No.117. Bangor Motive Power Yard, August, 1964. Bangor's 60ft turntable was located overlooking Caernarvon Road, so much so that a Britannia Class pacific overhung the road to the consternation of the uninitiated. Here Jubilee Class 4-6-0 No.**45600** *Bermuda* rotates on the vacuum assisted turntable whilst the traincrew stand and watch. *Norman Kneale.*

No.121. Bangor West End. 21st August 1966. Towards the end of steam, 'foreign' engines travelled over Regions other than their normal stamping grounds. Here Class A1 No.**60532** *Blue Peter* steams through Bangor station on the Down Fast line, seen here from No.2. signal box, with the Holyhead and Brymbo Special.
Norman Kneale.

No.122. Bangor West End. 21st August 1966. Seconds later, No.**60532** *Blue Peter* rolls towards Belmont Tunnel with the working. This impressive view, taken from No.2. signal box, shows the restricted space available when the cabin was re-sited in 1924. *Norman Kneale.*

No.120. (left) **Bangor, c.1963.** Another rarely mentioned member of the staff, the Guard, sometimes travelled on the footplate to take up their duties, in this case at Menai Bridge. Footplate hospitality frequently extended to other members of the travelling team, and William Alun Jones enjoys a lid of tea from the inevitable brew can, a semi-permanent fixture found on the tray above the firehole door. *Norman Kneale.*

No.123. Bangor East End. Summer 1962. Class 5 4-6-0 No.**45223** pulls away from the Up platform with a Class 1 working to Chester, comprised mainly of BR Standard Mark 1 stock. Above the signal cabin roof a 2-6-4T stands on the Down fast line, setting back to the shed after pulling into the up Passenger Loop platform with a local working from Afonwen. Assorted stock stands in both the Down platforms.   *Norman Kneale.*

No.124. Bangor. Carriage Landing Siding. Spring 1962. For most of the day a locomotive stood by as Up Side Passenger Shunt. Afternoons this duty was undertaken by whatever engine came in on the Horse and Carriage working between Holyhead and Ordsall Lane, and could range from a Class 4 to a Pacific. The morning duty was rostered to a 2-6-2T which turned out about 6.00am and worked as required until mid day. When not required it stood in the carriage landing siding, seen here behind No.1 platform and in front of the Parcels Office in the forecourt. No.**41234** was a regular performer on this duty.
Norman Kneale.

No.125. Bangor Station. 1965. An evocative scene, taken outside No.2 signal box in the six foot and looking up the centre roads towards the station and Chester. The Motive Power depot is devoid of locomotives, although a few wagons lurk on No.6 shed road and assorted stock occupies the sidings between the shed and the goods warehouse. Notice the good stock of coal outside the signal box steps. No more would the odd lump 'fall' off the footplate to supplement the signalman's dwindling supplies. The station layout remained unchanged for a short while, but eventually the Up Passenger and Goods Loop lines were taken out of use and removed. The footbridge from the Down platform to the Engineers Yard was also dismantled, the shed water tank was demolished and the Engineers Yard sidings reduced to but two lines. *Norman Kneale.*

No.126. Bangor. Summer 1962. A typical summer Saturday morning at Bangor. The Up 'Horse & Carriage' for Willesden stands in the Up Good Loop line, whilst a Fairburn 2-6-4T stands at the head of the 8.00am Parcels from Chester. A Class 5 stands on stock on the Carriage Siding whilst another Class 5 pulls slowly out of the Motive power yard and into the neck. *Norman Kneale.*

127. Bangor Locomotive Staff. 1896.

1.	T. Butler (Welsh Int. Footballer)	12.	S. Jones	23.	W. Pritchard
2.	R. Prytherch	13.	J. Williams	24.	H. Williams
3.	J.T. Edwards	14.	J. Barnett	25.	W.J. Hobbins
4.	T.J. Williams	15.	H.C. Hughes (D.L.S. Bescot, 1945)	26.	E. Williams
5.	J.R. Smith	16.	W.S. Williams	27.	J. Barnett (Night Foreman)
6.	R. Williams	17.		28.	R. Jones
7.	W. Davies	18.	A. Brown	29.	Ll. Rowlands
8.	J. Davies	19.	J. Prytherch	30.	R. Owen
9.	R. Jones	20.	W.A. Jones (R.S.F.)	31.	T. Pritchard
10.	H. Williams	21.	J.D. Carr	32.	R. Davies
11.	T.J. Wallace	22.		33.	W. Read
				33a.	H. Williams

34.	J. Roberts	46.	S. Jones
35.	H. Jones	47.	J. Roberts
36.	J. Thomas	48.	J. Gilbright
37.	W.O. Parry	49.	G. Owen
38.	W. Fox	50.	J. Jones
39.	S. Billington	51.	W.T. Davies
40.	D.T. Williams	52.	Meth. Owen
41.	J. Parry	53.	O. Williams
42.	Rt. Thomas	54.	W. Brown
43.	P. Cook	55.	T. Short
44.	W. Pritchard	56.	T. Coulter
45.	G. Jones	57.	W. Roberts